EMPOWERING THE MODERN WITCH

3-IN-1 BEGINNER'S GUIDE TO WITCHCRAFT, MEDITATIONS FOR PSYCHICS & EMPATHS, AND PROTECTION & REVERSAL MAGICK - INCLUDES 33 ESSENTIAL SPELLS, EXERCISES, AND RITUALS

LAUREL KELLY

RMC PUBLISHERS

RMC Publishers

© Copyright 2023 - All rights reserved.

It is not legal to reproduce, duplicate, or transmit any part of this document in either electronic means or in printed format. Recording of this publication is strictly prohibited and any storage of this document is not allowed unless with written permission from the publisher except for the use of brief quotations in a book review.

Table of Contents

Introduction — vii

Book One
The Practical Witch's Beginner Spellbook

Introduction — 3

1. WHAT IS WITCHCRAFT? — 5
   - History of Witchcraft — 5
   - Myths about Modern Witchcraft — 8
   - Purpose of witchcraft — 9
   - Famous Witches — 10
   - Magic or Magick? — 11

2. TYPES OF WITCHCRAFT — 13
   - Ceremonial Magic — 14
   - Covens — 14
   - Crystal and Gemstone Witchcraft — 14
   - Astrology — 16
   - Green Witchcraft — 18
   - White Witchcraft — 21
   - Chaos Magic — 21
   - Sigils and Rune Magic — 21
   - Divination and Numerology — 23
   - Other Types of Witchcraft — 25

3. EXPRESSING YOUR ENERGY AND TRIGGERING MAGICAL EFFECTS — 27
   - What is a spell? — 27
   - Parts of a Spell — 29
   - Common Spell Ingredients — 31
   - Why do Spells Fail — 33

4. 11 ESSENTIAL BEGINNER SPELLS ... 35
   Spell for Sleep ... 36
   Help from your Spirit Guide ... 37
   Quick Luck Spell ... 38
   Attraction or Remembrance Spell ... 40
   Releasing the Past ... 42
   Healing Spell ... 44
   Money Spell ... 46
   Herbal Remedies for Emotional Distress ... 48
   Patience ... 50
   Confidence Spell ... 52
   Basic Sigils or Bind Runes ... 54

5. CONCLUSION ... 59

Book Two
Meditations for Empaths and Psychics

Introduction ... 63

6. AM I AN EMPATH? ... 65
   What is a Psychic Empath ... 66
   Signs of Being a Psychic Empath ... 67
   What Psychic Abilities Exist? ... 68
   Why Everyone Should Develop Their Psychic Potential ... 69

7. DEVELOPING YOUR ABILITIES ... 71

8. AVOIDING NEGATIVE ENERGY ... 75
   Grounding ... 75
   Centering ... 76
   Shielding ... 76
   Avoidance ... 77

9. 11 MEDITATIONS FOR EMPATHS AND PSYCHICS ... 79
   Candle meditation ... 81
   Building Focus and Concentration ... 83
   Strengthening Intuition ... 86
   Building Empathy ... 88
   Connecting to your Spirit Guide ... 91

Kundalini - Basic Mantras	93
Alpha to Theta	96
Opening Chakras to Energy Flow	99
Enhancing Intuition and Clairvoyance	101
Psychic Development	103
Manifest Your Purpose	105
10. CONCLUSION	107
Affirmations for Empaths and Psychics	107

BOOK THREE
PROTECTION AND REVERSAL SPELLS

Introduction	111
11. CURSES AND HEXES	113
Psychic attacks	114
12. DISPELLING BLACK MAGIC AND NEGATIVE ENERGY	115
Types of Protection Spells and Traditional Cures	115
Reversal magic	116
Setting Boundaries	117
Boundary spells and symbols	117
Visualization and Affirmations	118
13. THE RULE OF THREEFOLD RETURN	119
14. 11 PROTECTION AND REVERSAL SPELLS	123
Preventative Protection Charms	124
Home Blessing	125
Banishment	127
Karmic Retribution	128
Clearing Negative Internal Thoughts	129
Recharge and Cleanse your Aura	131
Requesting Protection from Psychic Attacks	132
Crystal Magic for Protection	133
Camouflage Spell	135
Grounded Reflection Spell	136
Protection and Reversal Mantras	137
15. CONCLUSION	139

Introduction

Welcome to *Empowering the Modern Witch*, where we will explore the world of witchcraft and take our first steps towards spiritual empowerment.

This collection is intended as an introduction to the practice of witchcraft and its unique way of viewing the world. There are so many different types, schools, and styles of witchcraft that it can be challenging for any beginner to identify the best starting point for themselves in this realm. Think of this book as a guide to help you with the first few steps along your journey, showing you many of the possible paths you could take. Knowing enough to have a destination in mind will make this journey that much more satisfying.

Discovering witchcraft is an equal measure of learning about the spiritual realm and occult practices as it is about internal discovery. Finding your true purpose, power, and the most compelling way for you to express it.

Book 1, 'The Practical Witch's Beginner Spellbook', will provide the context around what modern witchcraft actually is and how it came

Introduction

into being. This introduction will also include some basic rituals and spells spread across different schools of witchcraft. This mix of different witchcraft styles will represent most of the major witchcraft practices, and the most common paths your journey could take.

Book 2, 'Meditations for Empaths and Psychics', includes guided meditations and exercises for the development of your psychic and empathic abilities. A key element of almost every aspect of witchcraft involves focusing your intention and being in a specific frame of mind. As mentioned earlier, this will be just as much an internal journey as an external one. Having some tools to help you focus and develop your mental prowess will be just as important as building up your book of spells and spiritual knowledge.

Book 3, 'Protection and Reversal Spells', specifically covers spells for reversing harmful magic and protecting yourself against dangerous energies. Many people turn to witchcraft because it feels like the universe or some other force is conspiring against them, and the first thing many new witches wish to learn is how to protect themselves from these external forces. Ensuring that you can safely use your newfound abilities will be the focus here. These more advanced spells will give you the tools you need to feel secure in your new practice.

I hope this collection will help you find what you are looking for, and that it will be only the first step in a lifelong pursuit of your true self.

> "Witchcraft is a way of life, a mystery tradition, a spiritual path. It is a celebration of life and the senses, a connection to the earth and the cycles of nature, and a honoring of the divine in all things."
>
> — Phyllis Curott, author and Wiccan priestess

Book One
The Practical Witch's Beginner Spellbook

Introduction

"Witchcraft is not only a tool for personal empowerment, it is a way of connecting with the divine, a way of tapping into the energy of the universe, and a way of living in harmony with the earth."

— Starhawk

Witchcraft is a broad term that can be used to describe many different things and has vastly different meanings and significance for different people. Throughout history and continuing today, there has never been one definition of witchcraft or what a witch is.

In some form or another, witchcraft has always existed, often shrouded in mystery or superstition. Ancient healers and medicine women, African witch doctors, Caribbean voodoo priestesses, and Old World pagan druids span cultures across the globe and millennia across time. Still, all represent the same thing: feminine power and spiritual connection, with secret knowledge and understanding guarded from outsiders and the uninitiated. For these

Introduction

same reasons, witchcraft has also been plagued by misconceptions and persecution.

This book will consider two main types of witchcraft practiced today: Wicca and Traditional Witchcraft. Wicca is a religion, while Traditional Witchcraft is not necessarily a religion and is more of an experience or way of life. Wicca is a modern practice that was founded in the 20th century based on studies of similar ancient traditions and beliefs modernized for the Western world. Traditional witchcraft is a term used to describe any form of witchcraft practiced before Wicca became popular and retaining more of its original form.

Rather than diving too deeply into Wicca and its many branches and variations, this book will focus more at Traditional Witchcraft. How these spiritual practices can be incorporated into your daily life, into your philosophy, and help you find a connection to your greater power and purpose on this Earth.

Use this book to guide you, to help find a practice of witchcraft that best suits your spiritual needs, or to develop your personalized practice.

What is Witchcraft?

History of Witchcraft

The term "witch" as we know it today, was coined in the 13th century and came from the Old English words "wicca" and "wicce", meaning sorcerer or wise woman. The earliest known use of this word is from around 1450, when it was used to describe older women who applied herbs and remedies to cure ailments.

But this is not the true origin of witches. Throughout history, women capable of wielding power or influence were often accused of using forbidden supernatural means. Originally these were related to roles of wise-woman or healers, but since biblical times these women were often misunderstood and persecuted. Accused of worshipping satan or other dark, forbidden beings, many early religious texts accuse women with deep spiritual connections of contacting the dead, divining prophecies, or other religious crimes.

In Western culture, organized religion has twisted the meaning of 'witch' into something sinister. While centuries of propaganda have created an ingrained belief that witchcraft is inherently evil or harmful, a modern feminist perspective shows that this was more related to the marginalization of single women, widows, and outsiders rather than witchcraft itself. That misconception still survives today. The first image that pops into people's heads when you say witch, or even Wicca, is most likely that of a social outcast or person who desires some unnatural and undeserved power.

With roots dating back to the most ancient civilizations, our definition of witchcraft will encompass any spiritual practice that uses rituals, spells, or supernatural tools to harness energy and deepen our connection to the world around us. Traditional witchcraft is a term used to describe a wide range of spiritual practices and beliefs rooted in pre-Christian, Indigenous, or cultural traditions. These beliefs and rituals slowly came into being over thousands of years and, as generation upon generation added to and refined that knowledge. These practices include rituals, spells, divination, and other forms of magic and may be associated with various deities, spirits, or ancestors. Traditional witchcraft also involves connecting to the natural world and using herbs, crystals, and other natural materials to strengthen this connection. The common thread throughout almost all traditional witchcraft is accessing a power greater than yourself to perform positive actions.

The true meaning and purpose behind Traditional Witchcraft have been obscured by male-dominated systems and cultures, which demonize female power, influence, and spirituality. Before the craze of witch-hunting swept Europe and later the Americas, women considered witches might have been midwives, herbalists, or traditional healers. They were providing valuable services for their community and acting as a strong thread in the social fabric. They worshipped pagan goddesses and understood the natural and supernatural world in a way incompatible with the advances of science and philosophy in Western society at the time. Possibly as a direct result of this, all of the major Christian religions have persecuted witches during their history.

It is important to note that the term "witchcraft" is often used in a broad and culturally specific way, and the practices and beliefs associated with traditional witchcraft can vary widely. Some people may practice traditional witchcraft as a form of spiritual exploration or personal growth. In contrast, others may use it to connect with their heritage or cultural traditions. It is important to respect the beliefs and practices of others and to be mindful of the potential risks and dangers involved in exploring unconventional or unfamiliar spiritual practices.

What is Paganism?

Often seen simply as the worship of nature, paganism is a broad term that refers to a diverse group of nature-based religions that often focus on worshipping a goddess and god and celebrating seasonal cycles and the natural world. Paganism has a long history but has undergone significant changes and evolution over time. Today, many people in modern society identify as Pagan and incorporate elements of Paganism into their spiritual practices, including witchcraft.

Paganism can take many forms, and there is no one way to practice Paganism. Some people may follow a specific tradition, such as Wicca or Druidry, while others may follow a more eclectic path and draw from various traditions and practices. Many Pagans focus on personal growth and spiritual development and may incorporate practices such as meditation, ritual, magic, and nature worship into their spiritual practices.

Paganism is a minority religion in many parts of the world but has a growing presence in modern society. Many Pagans are active in their communities and work to raise awareness about Paganism and promote understanding and acceptance of diverse spiritual paths.

Myths about Modern Witchcraft

You probably have heard or even believed some of the following myths about witchcraft. While most are harmless, myths and rumors detract from the true nature of witchcraft and can also discourage people from exploring it fully for themselves.

One of the most persistent myths about witchcraft is an association with the devil or engaging in black magic. While not all witches behave altruistically or according to the principles of Traditional Witchcraft at all times, modern witchcraft is intended as a positive and uplifting practice centered around strengthening connections between people, nature, and the divine. It celebrates life rather than seeking to harm others or achieve personal gain.

Another common myth is that only certain people are capable of practicing witchcraft or that you need some innate natural magical talent. In reality, witchcraft is a practice that is open to anyone interested in learning and growing, regardless of their background or experience. All it requires is an open mind and a willingness to learn. While not everyone starts from the same place, everyone can learn witchcraft and develop their skills.

There is also a belief that witchcraft is only for women. While women have traditionally played a dominant role in the practice and have been keepers of this knowledge, many witchcraft communities welcome men and do not discriminate based on gender.

What is Witchcraft?

Witchcraft has become increasingly inclusive and welcoming to anyone naturally drawn to exploring it.

Finally, some people believe witchcraft is only about casting spells and performing rituals, but this is just the external side of the practice. Witchcraft is also about developing deeper internal connections and abilities within yourself. Exploring your spirituality, understanding your true purpose, and using your inner power to change your life and the world around you positively.

Purpose of Witchcraft

That brings us to the purpose of witchcraft. There are several reasons you started reading this book. Plain old curiosity, a deeper desire to control or improve your surroundings, or a subconscious pull you can't explain. Every witch has a story to tell, of that moment when they realized this was the path they needed to follow, this was the place where the answers they sought were hiding.

And while it may not be a satisfying answer, the purpose of witchcraft and the deeper philosophy behind Traditional Witchcraft is the necessity of that search for those answers. Discovering your true purpose and place in the universe *is* the deeper purpose behind witchcraft. The details of that purpose and the answer to this question are unique for everyone, and the search for this answer is the essence behind all of the spells, rituals, and ceremonies.

By starting this journey, you are committing not only to harnessing your internal power, discovering the secrets that lie beyond Western science, and changing yourself for the better: but you are also committing to finding your true purpose. For most of us, this will be a long journey that requires confronting challenging thoughts and considerable courage. But if you can follow through, you will become a stronger person—someone who understands their place and how they fit into the universe.

Famous Witches

Here are a few of the more famous witches from the Western world you should know about as you start your journey. Their stories are powerful and deserving of their own books, and it would be worthwhile to seek out biographies of these individuals.

The Witch of Endor is the first written account of a witch described in the Hebrew Bible. She summoned the prophet Samuel from the afterlife.

Bridget Bishop was the first woman executed during the Salem witch trials in 1692, accused of bewitching five young women.

Marie Laveau was a voodoo priestess from 18th-century New Orleans. She supplied spells for all manner of people across all social classes in the city and was well respected for her abilities.

Gerald Gardner is the founder of the modern version of Wicca. He did not create Wicca himself, but he did bring much of the secret knowledge held by existing covens of witches to the attention of the public, and his actions have made the expansion of these beliefs possible, for better or worse.

Sybil Leek, Britain's most famous witch, considered herself the successor to Aleister Crowley, a magician, and scholar of the occult.

What is Witchcraft?

Magic or Magick?

In the witch community, you may see some controversy over the proper spelling of the word 'magic' or 'magick'. The traditional definition of 'magic' refers to tricks and illusions used for entertainment. Witches often prefer to use the spelling 'magick' to distinguish their actions and beliefs from stage magicians. Magick is any act that brings someone closer to their true purpose and is not necessarily supernatural. Many established Wicca communities use the term magick, but there is no need to conform to strict definitions or get into arguments about spelling. There is no right or wrong way, and choose whatever spelling you prefer. If you know the intention behind your actions and have the goal of fulfilling your true purpose, that is what is important.

This might seem like a small distinction and a minor argument, but it illustrates a larger point well. As you find your place in this new community, you may also find other small details taken very seriously. Come in with an open mind, ask questions, and be respectful, knowing there may be deeper reasons for these small details that some witches feel very strongly.

Types of Witchcraft

The various schools of witchcraft are distinguished by their underlying philosophies, tools, and rituals they use. You will see some common themes and patterns between them, and the core tenet of witchcraft, 'harnessing your inner power to be a positive force for good, while discovering your true self', is always present.

There is no best type of witchcraft, only the type that most resonates with your energy and speaks most truly to your soul. It is OK to experiment with different kinds of witchcraft when you are starting. Many new witches will find themselves naturally drawn to specific materials or rituals, and learning to follow this intuition and let it guide you is a fundamental early lesson for any witch.

For most witches, having a basic understanding of several of these main schools will help guide them on their journey. After all, if we don't know a path exists, how can we choose to follow it or not follow it? However, it can take years of time and dedication to master each type of witchcraft, and combining the deeper truths of multiple types of witchcraft is the mark of a true master and not something to be taken on lightly.

Ceremonial Magic

This is a good place to start if you can find a teacher since ceremonial magic derives from divine tradition and requires the presence of an experienced leader, such as a priest, priestess, or shaman who already knows and understands the rituals or ceremonies being used. If you want to be part of a larger community and have others help guide you, this is the perfect avenue to explore.

Covens

A coven is a group or community of like-minded witches. They will usually follow the same beliefs or practices, but what is more important is their common goals. By uniting their intention for a greater purpose, covens can create more powerful spells with wider-ranging and longer-lasting outcomes. Covens often rely strongly on traditions, rituals, and ceremonies as a tool to create harmony and bind the intention of all of their members.

How a specific coven operates is usually deeply held secret knowledge, and it will take time to become established as a witch. Details of a coven's ceremonies and practices are kept from outsiders, and it may take years to develop relationships and build trust before you are entrusted with a coven's knowledge.

Crystal and Gemstone Witchcraft

Stones, minerals, crystals, and gemstones represent a deeper connection with the Earth. These objects appear lifeless but simply

Types of Witchcraft

resonate more slowly, with vibrations attuned to a geological timescale rather than the fast-paced frequencies of plant and animal life. Crystal witchcraft is often associated with internal physical and emotional healing, calm, and deeper meaning or understanding.

These slower energies are less obvious but can be extremely powerful, leading to more profound spiritual knowledge and connection with cosmic understanding. The ability to attune your mind with forces that have existed since the dawn of time can grant a level of peace and wisdom that other forms of witchcraft may find difficult to achieve.

There are countless different materials to become familiar with as a crystal witch. While many are well-known, common, and easy to find, there are also many rare and hard-to-find crystals, gems, and minerals to seek out. A crystal witch always has new tools to track down and unique combinations of earth elements to discover. The crystals are used to attune your mind to the vibrations associated with the intention behind the spell. Understanding the deeper, slower purpose behind a spell will allow you to select the appropriate crystal to align your intention with the natural vibration of the spell's energy.

To start as a crystal witch, here is a list of materials to seek out and begin your collection of magical tools. Quartz is readily available, not too expensive, and has various forms that make it a great choice for creating a set of crystals for a new witch.

Clear Quartz represents purity and is essential for any witch as it has no set vibration frequency. Instead, clear quartz magnifies the energy of other magical implements, including herbs, sigils, or incantations. Focusing any energy into clear quartz to boost a spell's power is an essential skill for a crystal witch.

Citrine is a yellow or orange form of quartz that resonates at a level suitable for divination and purification. Adding orange citrine to a divination ritual can help you interpret visions of the future or hidden truths. A common use of yellow citrine is purifying other magical tools and removing negative energies.

Rose quartz is a bright red form of quartz that is emotionally charged. Spells for relationships, love, or friendship can all benefit from the addition of rose quartz.

Amethyst, the final variant of quartz, ranging from light to dark purple in color. Amethyst is excellent for developing psychic abilities or maintaining focus during meditation, tuned to the frequencies of the mind and third eye. Amethyst is also used in spells and rituals related to dreams.

Other elements which you should prioritize include **amber** (connecting with the sun and earth), **obsidian** (protection, overcoming obstacles, and divination), and **moonstone** (dreaming and intuition).

Astrology

While you may consider astrology a different skill outside of witchcraft, many traditional witchcraft practices incorporate elements of astrology. Astrology is a type of celestial magic and the most popular form in use today.

Understanding the signs of the Zodiac, the importance of lunar phases, houses of Astrology, and the significance of planetary alignment are all useful skills and, when combined, allow for deeper and more complex meanings to be interpreted by those willing to learn the details and intricacies of this form of witchcraft.

Types of Witchcraft

There is a depth and complexity of knowledge here, and it can take years to master the interpretation of all these related elements. However, any witch can benefit from a basic understanding of astrology by timing important spells and rituals with celestial events to improve the effectiveness of their magic. If you focus your knowledge in this area, you will understand how to align your actions with your true purpose, the stars, and fate itself.

Here is a short version of how your astrological birth sign may influence what type of witchcraft you are best suited for:

Aries: Storm Witch, able to influence and predict weather and other natural phenomena

Taurus: Animal Spirit, friend to living things, and can call upon wildlife for aid

Gemini: Fairy Witch, able to see and connect with magical creatures

Cancer: Hearth Witch specializing in protection spells

Leo: Worshiper of Goddesses, able to connect with higher powers

Virgo: Green Witch with an innate connection to nature

Libra: White Witch with strong love and relationship spells

Scorpio: Spirit Witch with a strong link to her spirit guide

Sagittarius: Hedge Witch, traveling effortlessly between realms with natural skills

Capricorn: Charm Witch, has a knack for creating and using magical implements

Aquarius: Chaos Witch, focused on results and outcomes or magic and does not rely on traditional rituals or ceremonies

Pisces: Sea Witch, connected with water and obtains energy from connection to the ocean, also able to brew strong potions

Green Witchcraft

Green witchcraft is about harnessing the power of the natural world and living things. Understanding and focusing the energy of the world around them in a way that benefits life and creates harmony where it is needed. Green witches can also be called by other names, like *Kitchen Witch* due to their use of herbs, or *Hedge Witch*, as their spells and rituals are often informal or improvised based on their instinctual knowledge of the natural world.

Throughout history, traditional healing methods have been used in many different cultures and societies around the world. These methods often involve natural remedies, such as herbs, diet, and physical therapies, and may be rooted in spiritual or cultural beliefs. Traditional healing methods may be used to treat a wide range of physical and emotional conditions and may be practiced by trained healers or practitioners.

Here are a few examples of traditional healing methods that have been used throughout history:

Ayurveda is a traditional medical system that originated in India and is based on the belief that health and wellness depend on a balance between the body, mind, and spirit. Ayurveda uses a variety of natural remedies, including herbs, diet, and physical therapies, to treat a wide range of conditions.

Traditional Chinese Medicine (or TCM) is a traditional medical system that originated in China and is based on the belief that the body's natural balance can be maintained or restored through natural remedies, such as herbs, acupuncture, and physical therapies.

Types of Witchcraft

Native American healing and African traditional medicine are traditions that involve the use of natural remedies, such as herbs, diet, and physical therapies, and may also involve spiritual or cultural practices. These traditions vary widely among different Native American tribes and African cultures.

It is important to note that traditional healing methods may not always be based on scientific evidence, and their safety and effectiveness can vary. It is always important to consult with a healthcare provider before using any form of treatment and to be aware of the potential risks and dangers of relying on traditional cures.

When creating spells or rituals, green witches usually rely on natural objects they have found or plants, whether wild or grown. The focus on green witchcraft is often healing or interpreting aspects of the natural world. Herbalism has deep ties to green witchcraft and is one of the green witches' most well-known tools.

Basic gardening skills are usually considered a requirement for becoming a green witch; however, they aren't necessary if you are just starting. If you haven't developed your green thumb yet, you could begin by foraging wild plants and ingredients. It may also take some time to learn this skill, but it will result in a greater understanding of how life grows and interacts, which is critical for a green witch.

Here is a list of common herbs and plants to get a green witchcraft garden started:

Amaranth repairs relationships

Basil cleanses negative energy

Bee balm attracts magical energy

Daisy for luck charms

Dandelion to use for sun rituals and attracting happiness

Garlic for protection spells

Heather dispels violent tendencies

Hyssop for purification and cleansing air

Lavender is used to create healing remedies

Lemon Balm for creating friendships

Marjoram eases grief

Mugwort harnesses lunar energy

Thyme helps with peaceful sleep

Witch Hazel strengthens divination rituals

Wormwood opens the mind for clairvoyance

Yarrow banishes fear and doubt

It is not necessary to create a comprehensive magic garden right away. You can slowly build up your collection of herbs, locations for harvesting wild plants, and recipes for spells over time as you gain more experience and deepen your connection with Mother Earth.

> "You are the sister to the wolf and friend to the hawk. You know in your heart the language of the plants and the songs of the wind. You have an innate connection to the wild edges. You know the beauty of the bee in flight, and hear the call of freedom on the horizon. And yet, as you go through your day today, it may be easy to miss the drumcall of the Earth."
>
> — WILD WOMAN BY ANNI DOULTER

Types of Witchcraft

White Witchcraft

There is no strict definition of a white witch or specific set of spells for white magic. What makes a white witch is intent. A focus on the greater good, a desire for the results of spells to benefit others, and a selfless, benevolent mindset are hallmarks of white witchcraft.

This can extend beyond the obvious, like an affinity for healing magic. White witches may also perform rituals for deepening social and spiritual bonds, craft protection spells for communities, and dispel negative energy from common spaces.

If your true purpose is serving others and the common good, becoming a white witch may be the best path for you.

Chaos Magic

Don't be scared off by the name, the focus of chaos magic is achieving specific outcomes or results, with less emphasis on the details of the ritual itself. If you feel more drawn to harnessing your intuition rather than learning ancient secrets, chaos magic might be an avenue worth exploring.

Or if you believe that the result is more important than the details of how you get there, you may be more naturally attuned to chaos magic.

Sigils and Rune Magic

A sigil is a symbol believed to have magical powers in some belief systems. Sigils are often used in magic rituals and spells and are believed to be able to focus the intention of the practitioner and bring about desired results. In some traditions, sigils are created by combining letters or other symbols in specific ways to represent a particular intention or goal. The sigil is then activated or charged during a ritual or spell and is believed to continue working on manifesting the desired outcome even after the ritual is completed.

Sigils are used in a variety of magical traditions, including chaos magic, ceremonial magic, and neopaganism. If interpreting and creating powerful imagery speaks to you, then sigils might be a form of witchcraft worth exploring. There are many forms of sigil magic; one popular today is rune magic. Here is a quick description of rune magic, and similar principles apply to other forms of magical sigils.

Runes are symbols often derived from Viking or Nordic history. These can be considered a type of sigil and can be used similarly as representations of physical or magical concepts. Rune magic is the process of combining runes and then representing or displaying them physically. Any spell which requires a sigil or visual representation of a concept can also use runes to a similar effect.

This process can become incredibly complex, and it is easy to get overwhelmed.

The best way to get started in rune magic is to learn the meanings behind individual runes. This may require some studying but is a necessary part of the process. There are 24 symbols in the oldest version of the Nordic alphabet, the Elder Futhark runes. You may also encounter other, newer versions of the runic alphabet with some additional runes, like Old English Futhorc or Younger Futhark.

Once you know the individual runes, you can think about ways to combine them. First, set your intention and focus on your goal, starting with small, short-term results. After you understand your aim, select runes that best reflect your desired outcome. Start simply, using two or three runes at most.

Bind runes combine two or more individual runes to represent a larger concept or entity. Stacked bind runes are drawn directly on each other and overlap and are used for manifesting. Same-stave runes are written along a common vertical axis to solve a specific problem. Radial bind runes emanate from a shared central point and are the basis for many protection or defense spells. Even advanced bind runes often don't require more than five runes.

The deeper meaning behind individual runes can be ambiguous, making it difficult to connect the meanings behind multiple runes into one cohesive concept. There is a lot of opportunity for growth and creativity here, and if you are naturally artistic or tend to think in images, finding a form of sigil magic may be a good path.

Divination and Numerology

Divination involves seeking knowledge from the future, often using methods incorporating chance or interpreting seemingly chaotic occurrences. For example, throwing a handful of runes onto a table so they land in a random pattern, then interpreting their order and meaning. Numerology is a popular form of witchcraft that can also be used for divination.

Numbers all have their own unique intrinsic energy and meaning. Numbers important to your life, such as your date of birth or address can provide insight into aspects of your character and your destiny. Depending on which numbers are selected, you can explore the future and destiny of specific events, relationships, businesses, or anything else that has a starting date or an associated numerical value.

The core idea behind numerology is that numbers hold spiritual and magical significance within them, with some numbers being more powerful than others. Different meanings or effects can be developed by combining numbers in different ways. Almost every form of magic ascribes intrinsic value to numbers, even if their specific interpretations differ. As an example, here is a method of determining your 'birth number':

First, write out your birth date as digits. If you were born on June 21, 1975, you would start with 6211975. Then, add all the individual digits together, 6+2+1+1+9+7+5 = 31. Then add those numbers together, 3+1 = 4, which gives a birth number of 4.

While different forms of Traditional Witchcraft may have different interpretations, here is an example of some of the meanings you might find for your birth number as a basic form of divination:

1: Signifies a connection to the universal life force. Since any number multiplied by one equals itself, it is considered a grounding number.

2: Relates to polarity or duality and indicates the balance in relationships between ourselves and the outside world.

3: Is typically considered the most magical number and is a symbol of action and interaction.

4: Represents the four elements, cardinal directions, and seasons. This is connected to creativity, compassion, and emotions.

5: Can be symbolic of the five human senses, the points of the pentagram, and is sometimes considered a bit chaotic. Five often indicates struggle and conflict.

6: Often associated with the sun, power, and strong masculine energy. Six is connected to responsibility and security.

Types of Witchcraft

7: Connected to lunar energy, femininity, intuition, and wisdom. Thought and consciousness are often represented by the number seven.

8: Connected to the planet Mercury, which relates to messages and divine communication. An eight flipped on its side is an infinity symbol.

9: Nine is three times three, which makes it a potent number in some systems and associated with goddesses, change, and growth.

0: Symbolizes the potential to form something new out of nothing, representing new beginnings and journeys.

Other Types of Witchcraft

This is only a sampling of the most popular forms of witchcraft. Hopefully, one of these has piqued your interest, but even if none of the above appealed to you, there is certainly some form of witchcraft out there that will speak to your inner magic and help you find your true purpose.

There is no one truth or answer out there, and while traditional witchcraft does have religious and spiritual components, there is no one source of truth. Whether you are a skeptic, believer, or somewhere in between, there will be a community for you.

Expressing Your Energy and Triggering Magical Effects

What is a spell?

While witchcraft is not all casting spells, an introduction to spells is a great place to start and get a feel for what Traditional Witchcraft feels like.

First, anything a witch does to create a magical effect can be considered a spell. You're probably most familiar with incantations, which are spells created using words and spoken out loud. However, other actions, like lighting a candle, drawing a sigil, or arranging crystals, can all be considered spells.

Spells are all about relationships, linking people, places, and things with different patterns of connection and, occasionally, severing those links. These links often start weak and require repetition to be reinforced gradually. Cyclic structures and patterns help with this reinforcement, which is why rhymes and repetitive actions are incorporated into spell casting. Different types of spells create and influence these connections in different ways.

A spell's exact nature and details influence its power, but the true source of power is your internal intention. Think of the details, the words of the incantation, the crystals or magical tools used, or the exact shapes of runes or sigils as tools to help focus that intention. While several different tools can be used to solve any problem, the most effective tool for the job depends on both the nature of the problem, as well as the skills and talents of the craftsperson.

While many covens and traditional Wiccan sources describe these spell components in great detail, we all interact with other spiritual realms differently and express our link with the spiritual realm differently. Any proven spell or one passed down through generations or within a coven will have a deeper meaning and power behind it, but it is possible to make modifications as needed.

Changing the words of an incantation can help you focus your intention based on your true path and beliefs. Using tools and materials readily available to you or with deeper personal meaning and unique ties to the metaphysical. Follow spell instructions as a guide, knowing that the true power of these spells comes from within yourself and any additional elements beyond your intention and focus are only there to guide you. Here are some of the major types of spells:

Correspondence spells create links between the physical world and the spirit world. This could involve communication with spirits in other realms.

Sympathetic spells create an attraction between forces. The principle behind sympathetic magic is that if you link two things in one realm, this connection will appear in other realms. Examples are spells to strengthen relationships between people.

Expressing Your Energy and Triggering Magical Effects

The reverse of sympathetic spells, *antipathy* spells, aims to sever a connection in the spiritual realm, weakening the existing relationship in the physical realm. This could be used to avoid unwanted attention or break ties with unwanted thoughts or behaviors.

Contagion spells are based on a similar concept, using objects and charms to represent a physical connection. The Law of Contagion states that touching another object or person creates a magical link to them, and you may wish to make, strengthen, or break such a link with spells.

Inversion spells are intended for protection against black magic or negative energy. They can either build up your spiritual immunity to these attacks or attempt to reflect the negative effects back at your attacker.

Parts of a Spell

Let's use incantations as an example to demonstrate the different parts of a spell.

An incantation is a series of words spoken or written as part of a magic ritual or spell. Incantations are often used to focus the intention of the practitioner and bring about desired results. In some belief systems, it is believed that the words and sounds of an incantation have a special power or energy that can influence the world in specific ways.

There is no set form or structure for an incantation, and the specific words and phrases used in an incantation may vary depending on the tradition or belief system. But some core elements will almost always be included in an incantation and most other types of spells:

- *Preparation* of materials, space, and physical self. This step corresponds to the spirit element.
- Achieving the correct *state of mind* for your mental self. This step corresponds to the air element.
- *Linking your intent* between the physical and spiritual realm will depend on whether the spell is for correspondence (connecting to the spirit world), sympathy (creating a connection), antipathy (severing a connection), or inversion (protection). This step corresponds to the water element.
- *Raising and directing energy* is necessary to fuel the spell; you will be using your internal energy and any assistance from deities, spirits, or magical tools and directing it with your focused intent. This step corresponds with the fire element.
- *Creating a channel between you and the target* can be done with magical tools or relying solely on your focused intent or proximity to the target. This step corresponds with the earth element.

Spells can be as simple as stating a short phrase or involve complex preparation and materials, with every element thoughtfully considered and planned in advance. Start simple, then add more complex elements as you become more experienced. There is no need for anything beyond the consideration of these five elements. Some common additional elements of incantations or other spells can also be included:

- The name or names of the deity or deities being invoked
- Words or phrases that are believed to have special power or energy, such as names of angels or deities, or words in ancient languages
- Repetitive phrases or word patterns that are believed to enhance or reinforce the power of the incantation

- Gestures or movements that are believed to add energy or power to the magic

As you become more advanced, you will quickly realize that many more potential elements can be considered when casting a spell. Two of the most important are the location and timing.

When choosing a location for the spell, it is important to remember that the physical world reflects the spiritual. Entrances reflect transitions and intersections between realms; therefore, locations such as doorways, windows, or other physical thresholds are places where the distance between the physical and other realms is closest, and spells can be more effective.

Other more metaphysical or abstract entrances and transitions can also be used. For example, dusk and dawn represent the transition between day and night, equinoxes between seasons, and even moon phases could be considered transitions in the physical realm. This is how timing can be incorporated into spellcasting. Wherever or whenever there is a threshold of change, the physical and spiritual worlds' influence on each other is strongest, and spells are more powerful.

Common Spell Ingredients

The only mandatory element that must be present in every spell is your focused intention. It is unnecessary to seek out exotic or rare spell components; everyday items can (and will) become magical through their use in spell creation. However, this should be done with caution, as enchanted tools maintain their magical energy. Once you intend to use an item for magical purposes, it should no longer be used for its former everyday purpose, as the energy instilled within it may express itself in unintended ways.

Here are some examples of magical tools that you may already be familiar with and should be able to find easily.

Crystals, metals, and gemstones represent the earth element, and the natural vibrations of crystals can connect us with the earth and help us tune in to healing frequencies. They can also supply any other specific colors or elements that could support your spell.

Tarot cards are well-known for their use in divination but require considerable knowledge to apply effectively.

Sigils are more than just magical symbols; you should think of them as magical shorthand, with all the intention and meaning behind a spell expressed by a simple but powerful image. These are helpful ways to keep focused while casting, as it's easier to keep a single image in your mind compared to a complex idea.

Colors have their magical energy, and using items of the appropriate color can enhance spells.

Numbers may seem abstract but can be easy to incorporate into spells using repetitions and duplicates of other tools (for example, by using three crystals or candles instead of one).

Herbs, plants, and flowers are associated with different magical effects and outcomes.

Grimoires (or book of shadows) are spell books that can record the specific details of your spells and help you personalize them. They will become magical through their use.

Combining these elements could involve, for instance, a specific number of flowers of the desired color, which can make spells more effective. However, these additional layers also add complexity and require much more focused intention to avoid unintended chaotic effects. Beginner witches should keep things simple, using a minimum number of enchanted objects, each with a singular focus and purpose. It is not necessary to consider every possible element and all of their combinations. For example, you don't need to worry if your crystal isn't the perfect color for the spell you are casting. Focus on the elements you have specifically considered and intentionally chosen to enhance your spell.

Why do Spells Fail

The first thing to remember is that, more often than not, a properly cast spell hasn't failed; it just has not been sufficiently reinforced. The initial effects may be so small that they go unnoticed, but gradual repetition strengthens and builds spiritual connections. Spells may also manifest results in unexpected ways. If your intention is set on an outcome or goal, there is no telling what path or journey the spirit realm will use to realize it.

On the other hand, the most important part of manifesting magic is the intention behind it. Spells created with a clearly defined purpose or a burning desire or need will usually succeed. It is not enough to casually want something. You must truly desire and need that outcome to occur, either for yourself or, ideally, for some larger purpose or other people.

Another factor is that it takes considerable practice to learn how to maintain concentration throughout the casting of an entire spell. You may find that your mind may wander, however briefly, even during a short incantation. If you have incorporated multiple tools or elements into a spell, trying to spread your intention between too many things will weaken it. This is why you should keep things simple in the beginning. Witchcraft is a skill that takes time to develop, and building up your capacity to focus your mind is the first step to becoming an effective witch.

The manifestation of a spell will reflect the emotional state of the caster at the time of the spell's creation. You may get extreme results if you are stressed, anxious, or experiencing powerful emotions. Achieving the desired result requires a focused mind, balanced spirit, and empathetic soul.

11 Essential Beginner Spells

These 11 spells will help you get started on your journey. They can all be cast without magical tools and only aim to accomplish outcomes achievable for a beginner witch. Select whichever speaks most to your true purpose, and modify them if necessary to better reflect your personality and style of witchcraft.

Even if the purpose of these spells does not reflect your original intention for learning witchcraft, you can think of them as useful exercises for building focus and intention during spell casting. Once you can easily cast these simple spells, you will know that you are ready to add additional complexity or find out which types of spells are more effective for you.

Spell for Sleep

This is a basic spell to help you sleep. Starting with a simple, straightforward purpose you can repeat regularly makes this a great spell for practicing and building your focus and intention.

To prepare, you can either imagine or picture a candle burning in your mind. Using an actual candle is not recommended for safety reasons.

Repeat the following three times as part of your night-time routine.

> *By this spell's flame, I will soundly sleep*
> *As day becomes night's, blackest deep*
>
> *Moonlight guide my peaceful dreams*
> *Under the watchful gaze of Selene*
>
> *As my flame falters, flickers, and dies*
> *Sweet rest will come to my weary eyes*

11 Essential Beginner Spells

Help from your Spirit Guide

This spell requests your guardian spirit to strengthen the bond between you and them or to aid you in a time of need. This is a way to practice invoking a greater power from the spirit realm, and what better power to start with than one that is already connected with you? A slightly more complex spell than the previous one since you will need to divide your focus between your intention and the talisman you select.

To prepare, select any object to become a talisman representing your guardian spirit. Hold it or place it nearby, whichever feels most comfortable.

Repeat the following incantation, and modify it as necessary to directly address your guardian spirit if you know their name or form. Your exact words are less important than having a focused intent behind them. If a phrase doesn't feel right or you want to modify something slightly, follow your intuition and make it personal.

Chaos surrounds me, as air becomes smoke
Therefore my guardian spirit, I hereby invoke

Grant me your wisdom, strength, and aid
So I may overcome the path fate has laid

By the goddesses and powers which cross between
I request that you reach through and soon intervene

Strengthen our bond and grant what I require
To save my true will from forces destructive and dire

Quick Luck Spell

Continuing to build on what we've learned so far, this spell requires some additional preparation and consideration of your location. The luck from this spell isn't specifically intended for you. Still, it can be targeted toward others—excellent practice for using witchcraft to benefit those around us and fulfill a larger purpose.

To prepare, you will inscribe three things into a candle: a name, the word luck, and a sigil or image representing luck, like a four-leaf clover. Use a toothpick, knife, or letter opener.

You should experiment a bit and find what works best for you. Remember, once you find a suitable object for inscribing candles, this will become a magical tool and should not be used for its original purpose anymore, so choose carefully.

The spell will last for as long as the candle burns. Do this from a central point where you would like luck to spread. Allow the candle to burn; as it does, it will gradually release the luck to the person named on the candle.

Keep the entrance to the room sealed to contain the luck for longer in that room, or open the entrances to allow the luck to flow out of the space and follow the named person for as long as the candle burns.

Once the three things have been inscribed, recite the following phrase before burning the candle.

With the burning of this wick
I call on Fortuna's white magick

Bless this name with good luck and chance
Guiding their true purpose to advance

In their favor wheels of fate shall turn
Whilst this sacred candle may burn

Attraction or Remembrance Spell

Let's practice using color. It's unnecessary to consider the color of every item involved in a spell. Just focus on the key magical items being used. For this attraction spell, select pink items where you can represent the person with whom you would like to create a connection. Flowers, candles, stones, anything the target of the spell has touched. Any of these items could be used to add pink to the spell.

To prepare, find a pink item and write the person's name on a small piece of paper. Fold the paper so that the name isn't visible. The tighter you fold the paper, the stronger the bond you want to create. A single loose fold to be briefly remembered in their thoughts, twice over for friendship, three tight folds for romantic interest. Place the folded paper under or within the pink object. *It is important to remember that witchcraft cannot be used to remove another autonomy and can only kindle pre-existing consensual feelings.*

This version of the spell is intended to create a new connection or attraction between people, using a link in the spirit realm to create a link in the physical realm. But there can be subtle differences between spells based on intent and action. By altering your intention's focus, you can subtly change the spell so that instead of creating a new connection, it can reinforce a weak link. Reopening lines of communication that have been severed, bringing understanding between people, or repairing existing relationships. This is an important lesson to remember, and fully understanding a spell's purpose is critical before you can effectively cast it.

Imagine the target of your spell, remain focused on the pink item, and repeat the following incantation three times. As this spell is repeated, the bond will naturally grow stronger at the level of intent set by the number of folds of the paper. You can invoke different goddesses based on your goals, whether it's love (Aphrodite), friendship (Philtres), or just remembrance (Mnemosyne).

Goddess _____,
Send thoughts of me into their mind
Flowing down into their heart

Place myself within their life
So that we may never part

Releasing the Past

This spell is the reflection of the previous spell and is used to break unwanted connections to people, places, or memories. Most spells focused on breaking a connection will create a symbolic representation of the link in the physical realm and destroy that as part of the spell. The simplest symbolic representation is simply writing a description of the link on a piece of paper and burning it. This is not an action to be taken lightly or without serious consideration.

The spell itself is simple, but it is a good exercise for your journey as a witch. How does removing this link to your history further your true purpose? Even if you choose not to cast this spell, understanding why you have made this choice may benefit you. And this is one of the strongest benefits that witches receive. It is not just knowing how to cast a spell. Understanding when not to cast a spell is equally important.

To prepare, write down the past event you want to remove your connection to on a piece of paper. If it involves another person, it could be their name, or the name of the place where the link was created. You will also need a lit candle. Use a white candle if the intent of the spell is to provide you strength, a pink candle to heal yourself, or a blue candle if it brings you peace. To start the spell, light the candle, then recite the following incantation:

In candle's light, remove what was before,
Release, renew, forevermore.

Set me free, release my chains,
My spirit unburdened, no longer it pains.

Move my path forward, towards a pure start
Remove that which does not serve my heart

In candle's light, find my strength to soar,
Release, renew, forevermore.

As you recite the incantation, imagine yourself waking confidently away from the past. Once you have finished repeating the spell, extinguish the candle and cross the nearest threshold.

Healing Spell

If you feel that your journey will take you on the path to becoming a white witch, this is an essential type of spell to become familiar with. Healing spells, even simple ones like these, are powerful and will require repetition and additional magical tools. This specific version of a healing spell will also give you a chance to try combining crystals with an incantation.

To prepare, place the three objects below in a triangle formation, repeating the following incantation three times for three nights in a row. This reinforces and creates the links needed for this healing spell. You can use a combination of the following objects: white candles, pieces of clear quartz, an object the target of the spell has touched (or their name written on a small piece of paper). If you don't have access to quartz yet, you can use an additional candle instead.

Light the candle and then as you recite the spell, focus your intention on the sick person and picture them healing and becoming well. The more detailed your focus and intention, the better; picture bones mending, illness leaving the body, or stress washing from their mind. The candles do not need to burn for long and can be reused. Repeat the ritual regularly (daily or weekly) until the individual is healed.

11 Essential Beginner Spells

Magic mend and candle burn,
Illness leave and health return.

Magic mend and candle burn,
Illness leave and health return.

Magic mend and candle burn,
Illness leave and health return.

Money Spell

While directly asking for financial gain may not necessarily align with the deeper philosophies of Wicca or Traditional Witchcraft, that is not what this spell is trying to accomplish. Control over your financial situation in the physical realm is necessary if you wish to pursue and move toward your true purpose.

Rather than simply asking for money, you are asking for guidance toward a path that will allow you to pursue deeper spiritual matters rather than focus only on your physical needs. This spell walks a fine line between asking fate for personal gain and asking for permission to seek out your truth. Walking this fine line with integrity is also an important skill to develop within yourself.

To keep building on some more advanced techniques, this spell can benefit from the use of specific herbs to focus the results.

To prepare, pick one of the following herbs or plants to use, crush it, and make an infusion of it in a bowl (steep it in hot water like tea) for three minutes, three times. Again, remember that the bowl you use will become a magical tool, and should only be used for magical purposes, so choose your tools with intention.

Here are some herbs to use. These are readily available for most people, but you will discover many more options if you pursue the path of a green witch:

Alfalfa to draw money directly to you

Bergamot or **Orange Mint** to support financial success

Pecan to obtain financial stability

Basil for attracting customers or clients to you or your business

11 Essential Beginner Spells

Lucky Hand Root to help find new employment

Wash your hands in the infusion and visualize the prosperity you desire. Recite the following incantation.

You will repeat this over three days, reinfusing the water in the bowl each time.

Prosperity and wealth, begin flowing to me
From worries and stress, I wish to be free

I seek no comfort or physical gain
Only absence of spiritual pain

Allow my whole spirit to fully pursue
The deeper purpose, of witches' true

Herbal Remedies for Emotional Distress

This is the first spell that isn't an incantation. This may not seem or feel like witchcraft the first time you try it, but green witchcraft involves creating herbal remedies or potions to achieve effects. Other forms of witchcraft also use spells that are not verbal in nature, so this is good practice to try something that isn't an incantation.

Creating your combination of plants, herbs, and oils and recording these recipes and their effectiveness is a Green Witches version of a spellbook. Try crafting a potion using one or more of the four herbs below as a starting point. Use your knowledge of what plants heal you and your loved ones to personalize your potion. While green witchcraft does require some outside knowledge, try to follow your intuition about what you, or the spell's target, needs and what would bring them back into balance.

While herbs can be a helpful addition to a self-care routine for managing emotional distress, it is important to remember that herbs are not a substitute for professional medical or mental health care. If you are experiencing serious physical or emotional distress, seeking support from a trusted healthcare provider is important. With that in mind, here are a few herbs that may help manage emotional distress:

Lavender is a calming herb often used to reduce anxiety and promote relaxation. It can be taken as a tea, applied topically as an essential oil, or taken in capsule form.

Chamomile is a calming herb often used to reduce anxiety and promote sleep. It can be taken as a tea or taken in capsule form.

St. John's Wort is a herb commonly used to treat mild to moderate depression. It is typically taken in capsule form.

Valerian Root is a herb widely used to promote relaxation and improve sleep. It can be taken as a tea or taken in capsule form.

Patience

Let's get back to more traditional incantations here. This spell for patience is strictly for the improvement of the self. It is not intended to help you wait for a future event. It is a spell focused on building up your internal strength.

The journey you are taking now is just as much internal as external, so let us try a spell to help you build yourself up and become your true self. This spell will call upon divine numbers, and you can enhance it by using multiple talismans or magical items, either in groups of three or eight.

To prepare, give yourself a set time free from distraction. While this is always important, it is critical not to be interrupted during this spell. You will repeat the following three times in a row. Focus on your breathing and attempt to speak the words as slowly and clearly as possible. Each repetition should be slower and more deliberate than the previous one.

This will become difficult, your mind may wander, and you may lose focus, and the words will run together and start to lose meaning. This is the longest incantation so far, and it will be a test of holding your intention for an extended time.

> *In spirit realms, where time is a dance,*
> *I weave a spell of patience, an enchanting trance.*
> *Through this cycle of eight, a sacred embrace,*
> *Patience takes root, its essence I trace.*
>
> *Through my will and intent, I power this spell,*
> *To nurture peace and endurance, where it may dwell.*
> *Infinite wisdom of numbers divine,*

Let patience bloom, like sacred vine.

With each breath, a rhythmic flow,
My patience grows, and I shall know,
The power of stillness, a sacred art,
Manifesting calm, a tranquil heart.

In the symphony of moments, I'll be still,
With patience as my guide, purpose I will fulfill.
Bound to the rhythm of cosmic design,
Patience, my virtue, forever shall shine.

Through steady steps, I journey along,
With patience as my guiding song.
No bounds, no limits, just serene flow,
Patience leads me, wherever I go.

With every breath, I find my center,
Patience, my ally, a gentle mentor.
In stillness and grace, I shall reside,
Patience, my strength, mirthful guide.

So let it be, this spell I weave,
Patience abundant, may it never leave.
In harmony with time, my spirit aligned,
With patience as my ally, I transcend unconfined.

The eighth verse, the cycle complete,
Patience has blossomed, a sacred feat.
With tranquil breath and steady heart,
I embrace patience, a work of art.

Confidence Spell

Another self-improvement spell, and another reflection of a previous spell. You will notice this pattern often in witchcraft, as most spells have a mirror or shadow spell with a seemingly opposite purpose. Balancing patience with the confidence to act when appropriate requires a finely-tuned intuition and understanding of the world around us. A person who has one of these skills without the other will feel out of balance or like they are missing some control over their life path. Anytime you decide to pursue a path of internal strength, remember to consider if you are creating an imbalance and use a mirror of that spell to keep your internal energy aligned.

Another skill this spell teaches is creating a shorthand magical language. It can be difficult to keep your intention focused, especially with complex spells. Having your own language to express your magical energy allows you to focus your intention on multiple concepts within a single spell. In this example, the confidence you feel from this spell will manifest a name, which can then be incorporated into other spells which require confidence to cast.

To prepare, breathe deeply, and visualize energy flowing into your body. Once your mind feels focused, take slow breaths, each deeper than the last, and draw energy into your body. You will feel it coursing through your body, and once it becomes difficult to sit still and you feel the urge to move, recite the following incantation. Once complete, speak the name of your inner power. Try repeating the spell on a different day if nothing comes to you. After your inner confidence has named itself, you can use that as shorthand in future spells. This name will be unique to you, and this shorthand form is important when building your grimoire. It will take time and potentially many repetitions before the name of your confidence reveals itself to you.

Ignite my spirit, let it burn bright,
From the depths of my soul, harness it's might.

Within my true self, set a blazing fire,
Unleash my strength, let it inspire.

I surge forward, a force untamed,
Embracing my power, let it be named.

Basic Sigils or Bind Runes

Now, we will build on the idea of a personal magical language and try creating a basic sigil. The benefit of sigils is that they can take a complex idea, which we would normally have to consciously focus on to describe and express it directly to our subconscious.

First, select a simple idea or concept you would like to use regularly. This could be from a previous spell, something like luck or attraction, or something else we haven't covered yet. While many existing sigils have been discovered throughout the history of Traditional Witchcraft, let's try creating our own. That means this will technically be a chaos sigil and our introduction to chaos magic. There is nothing inherently sinister about chaos magic. It is more about following your intuition and creating your own spells based on your intention.

Next, create a sentence or short phrase that expresses your desired outcome of that spell. Make this as short as possible, with no unnecessary words or details. The sigil will be a visual representation of this desired outcome and the shorter the phrase, the simpler and more recognizable the sigil will be to your subconscious.

The construction phase follows, and the simplest method is to physically draw the sigil. For a short-duration or temporary spell, a pencil and a piece of paper will work, but for a more permanent spell, you may need something more durable. Carvings in wood and etchings in metal will work as more permanent sigils, but it would be prudent to start with some temporary sigils to practice at this stage. As the temporary sigil fades over time, and the power of the spell will also dwindle and need to be cast. Once you have selected the appropriate materials, you can generate the sigil.

First, write down the entire sentence or phrase you created. Then remove all of the vowels and repeated letters. Use the remaining letters to create an abstract symbol. Combining, rotating, and layering the letters as you see fit. Keep things as simple as possible, so you can recreate the sigil as desired. This process can take time and several attempts. Meditation or deep breathing exercises might be necessary to put yourself into the right mental state to create the sigil.

Once you have decided on a design and know you will construct it, you can inscribe the sigil onto something.

Finally, the sigil should be placed near the target of the spell.

A similar process is used for crafting bind runes. Instead of using words and letters, you start with runes, each with their own intrinsic meaning. After selecting which nordic alphabet you wish to use, and learning the meaning behind the symbol, you can get started.

Draw out the runes in the format that aligns best with your intended purpose. There is no set method here, and it is often best to keep drawing multiple arrangements of the runes. Do this with a clear mind and let your subconscious guide the process, drafting out different patterns and combinations as they come forth in your mind. Runes can be turned, flipped, or mirrored to make them align with each other; however, this can also change their purpose and intention. The process of creating a powerful and meaningful design will take time, and it is recommended to take breaks and rest to let your mind clear. Often, the selection of the ideal bind rune will come to you in the form of a thought or dream hours or days after sketching a series of drafts.

It is important to inspect your selected design carefully. Many runes appear similar, and stacked bind runes can often create new, hidden runes within them. Carefully review your design and check for hidden, mirrored, or other unexpected meanings.

The final step is to create a physical representation of your bind rune. For short-term spells, simply being drawn on paper with intention may be sufficient, but to create more powerful or permanent spells, the bind runes may need to be carved into wood or stone. Choose materials that reflect and represent the deeper intention and meaning of the spell and which can be placed appropriately. For example, a luck spell could be inscribed onto a necklace or pendant, or a home protection spell could be displayed as a piece of meaningful artwork on your walls.

During the actual creation of the physical rune, it is important to focus on your intent and keep the purpose of the spell at the forefront of your mind. As you carve, draw, or paint the individual runes, you should also consider their meaning and how they will contribute to the overall spell. This can be a mentally taxing and long process, especially if you create long-term bind runes for more permanent effects over multiple hours. Starting small, with simple bind runes that can be created over 10 to 15 minutes, is recommended for beginners until they develop the focus and practice needed to craft more elaborate and demanding runes.

Keep the finished bind rune close to you or the intended target and in a prominent or visible position. If the intended effect is only temporary, or you have received the outcome you desired, then the bind rune has fulfilled its purpose and should be destroyed.

Burning (paper or wood) or burying (stone) are both good options for ending bind rune spells.

Conclusion

Congratulations, you have taken your first steps on your journey into the world of Traditional Witchcraft. You will probably have noticed by now that some of those beginner spells resonated with you more than others, or you may have been drawn to certain spellcasting methods.

These feelings can help guide the next steps of your journey, so you can begin to create a vision of your future and how you will use witchcraft to become your true self and awaken your power. While this journey is different for everyone, I hope these first steps have been helpful and that you continue with me to discover even more about what lies beyond our senses.

Book Two
Meditations for Empaths and Psychics

Introduction

Whether new to meditation or not, this book will help you develop mental skills and abilities that will help you on your journey as an empath or psychic. But before we get started, please remember that these are not traditional meditations intended to help clear your mind, relax, or destress. These exercises will either put you into a specific mental state, which is more in tune with the psychic energies around you, help you develop specific skills, or increase your ability to maintain focus and concentration. They require attention and intense focus and will require some effort to follow correctly.

Rather than calm and relaxation, we are seeking attunement and awareness. Practicing the skill of meditation will develop your intuition and give you the ability to access your inner knowledge and understanding more easily. Psychics and empaths do not rely on their five senses and logic to understand and experience the world around them; they have other natural and eventually trained skills to give them a complete picture of the universe. The more you build and develop these skills, the more your natural talent and potential will benefit you and those around you, either by sensing

INTRODUCTION

energies in others more accurately or blocking unwanted energy more effectively.

These meditations are typically only 5 minutes long but those will be a focused and intense for 5 minutes with a clear goal and purpose. As you may already know, keeping your mind focused on a specific thought for this long sounds easy but can be difficult without practice. You can extend these meditations even further as you continue to use them. However, if you cannot maintain focus for the full 5-minute meditation right away, that is completely normal. Part of developing psychic energy is building up your natural attunement to the spiritual world in all waking moments, or your baseline state of psychic awareness. You also build your maximum potential when focused and intentionally sending or receiving energy.

Am I an Empath?

Empaths are individuals who have the ability to sense and deeply understand the emotions and experiences of others. This can be a powerful gift, but it can also be a challenging burden, as empaths may absorb the emotions of others and struggle with setting boundaries. Being bombarded by negative emotions from others in certain situations or environments can make life difficult for empaths. A similar group to empaths is Highly Sensitive People.

Highly sensitive people (HSPs) have a heightened sensitivity to their environment and the emotions and experiences of others. HSPs may be easily overwhelmed by stimuli and struggle with setting boundaries. Here are a few coping skills that may be helpful for empaths and HSPs to practice:

Identify and understand your sensitivity: It can be helpful for empaths and HSPs to appreciate their sensitivity and recognize how it affects them. This can involve seeking resources and information to learn about your triggers and needs.

Practice self-care: Empaths and HSPs must take care of their physical and emotional well-being. This can involve setting aside time for rest and relaxation, engaging in activities that nourish the soul, and finding ways to manage stress. Meditation and spending time in nature are two effective and simple options.

Set boundaries: It can be helpful to set boundaries to protect their energy and well-being. This can involve saying no to requests or invitations that are not in alignment with your values or needs or setting limits on the amount of time you spend in stimulating or overwhelming environments.

Engage in activities that allow for self-expression: Empaths and HSPs may find it helpful to engage in activities that allow for self-expression, such as writing, art, or music, to process and understand their emotions and experiences.

Find support: Seeking help from trusted friends, family members, or professionals to process and manage their emotions and experiences.

Protect your energy: if you are familiar with the basics of traditional healing practices or witchcraft, you can use magical tools like crystals to protect your energy, techniques like smudging to purify yourself, or sigils to cast basic healing and rest spells.

What is a Psychic Empath

Empath is a term used in psychology, referring to anyone who feels a higher-than-normal level of empathy for others. This is the western science definition, but it is not the only type of empath. A psychic empath is different, and in addition to that same heightened feeling of empathy, they also channels the emotions and experiences of others. Often called 'emotional resonance,' in many psychic empaths, this is an unconscious and often uncontrolled ability. At the same time, there are many benefits to knowing what others are feeling and having a higher-than-normal level of empathy, such as connecting emotionally and providing support to others more easily. Psychic empaths can use their abilities to detect subtle changes in the energy of others, making them skilled in techniques like reiki, spiritual healing, and mediumship.

On the other hand, there are some serious drawbacks. As you are probably already aware or can easily imagine, constantly seeing and feeling the emotions of those around you is incredibly draining and can take an emotional, physical, and spiritual toll on you. Being aware of the pain and distress of loved ones is very different from channeling those feelings and experiencing them yourself. The struggle of separating your emotions from others and being drained from absorbing the negative energies around you can make everyday life challenging.

There are also different types of psychic empaths, which you could imagine as channeling various aspects of the spiritual energy surrounding all of us. Some channel the physical, feeling touch and pain. Others channel emotions, experiencing feelings and mental states. Less common types of psychic empaths channel dreams or energies from animals or plants.

Signs of Being a Psychic Empath

There is no strict definition or diagnosis for who is or isn't a psychic empath. While some of us channel the emotions of others without effort, some have to develop this skill through practice. The following are general indications that you may be a psychic empath:

You prefer being alone: Many psychic empaths are introverts and need time to recuperate after being around others or in crowds.

You have mood swings: Channeling emotions and energies from others will alter your emotions if you are not careful or have not developed your defenses. Unpredictable changes in your mental state are a sign you may be unknowingly channeling psychic energy.

You value your emotions: If you feel that emotions are important and appreciate understanding your and others' emotions, that is a sign you may have empathic ability.

You are sensitive to chaos: Being distressed by randomness, unpredictability, and lack of control is a feeling many untrained psychic empaths feel.

You are drawn to ancient cultures and the paranormal: An innate understanding that there is more to this world than can be explained, and a connection to the spirit realm can sometimes show up in people this way.

You are intuitive: Sometimes, you know things and can't explain how or why.

What Psychic Abilities Exist?

A psychic can sense beyond the physical world, experiencing the intangible as emotional, physical, or spiritual impressions. While almost everyone has some innate psychic ability, most practicing psychics have a higher natural affinity. However, we can all benefit from building our intuition and learning to understand what our minds are trying to tell us.

Psychic abilities can manifest in many different ways. Still, we can generally group them into four different categories or methods of sensing. Some psychics only have one form of sensing at first and develop the others over time with practice.

Clairvoyance is seeing visuals, images, or scenes in your mind. These images are often metaphorical and can be difficult to interpret at first. Seeing auras or visions of the future are also types of clairvoyance.

Clairaudience is hearing messages, almost always as someone speaking directly into your mind. Unlike clairvoyance, these messages are typically short and straight to the point, requiring less interpretation.

Clairsentience is the most common psychic ability and is expressed as a feeling or intuition. This is similar to psychic intuition and manifests as experiencing the emotions, physical sensations, or experiences of those around you.

Claircognizance is the ability to understand information directly from intuition. Think of it as an advanced version of intuition, where cause and effect or specific details are known solely from the psychic energy channeled from others.

Why Everyone Should Develop Their Psychic Potential

Even if you have no desire to perform readings or help others with your skills, developing this part of your mind can benefit anyone. Over time, your psychic abilities will become a source of kindness, compassion, and creativity that will improve every aspect of your life.

Psychics are also innate problem solvers, seeing links and solutions others can't recognize. They become leaders by more easily forming strong bonds with others. They can more easily go into a state of lucid dreaming, gaining control over their subconscious.

There are also downsides to having psychic abilities. However, these are typically the result of a person with high psychic potential not properly developing or training their gifts. Common mental health concerns for psychically attuned individuals include an inability to say no to others or set boundaries, difficulty working with screens or electronics, a higher risk of addiction, feelings of fatigue and tiredness, and depression or anxiety. Most of those symptoms result from the increased effort required to process the extra-sensory input being received almost constantly. They can likely be resolved by developing defensive mental skills through practice and meditation.

Developing Your Abilities

The focus of developing psychic abilities is centred around your third eye or Ajna chakra. Strengthening your third eye will improve your internal psychic abilities, like intuition, and your external psychic abilities. Once you have cultivated the ability to listen to the inner wisdom of your third eye, it will help you understand not only your motivations but also give you insight into others.

The term 'third eye' generally refers to a spiritual concept that represents an inner vision or insight that is beyond the physical senses. It is often associated with the pineal gland, a small endocrine gland in the brain. It produces the hormone melatonin, which helps regulate sleep-wake cycles. In spiritual traditions, the third eye is sometimes associated with higher consciousness and enlightenment. It is believed to be a gateway to spiritual knowledge and understanding.

In some traditions, the third eye is thought to be connected to the Ajna chakra, or the 'command' chakra, which is located between the eyebrows. It is believed to be a center of psychic powers and spiritual insight. It is associated with the sense of perception and the ability to see beyond the physical realm.

The concept of the third eye is found in many different spiritual traditions. It is often depicted as a symbol of enlightenment or inner wisdom. Activating or opening the third eye can bring about spiritual growth and a deeper understanding of the self and the world.

Inner knowing will help you make better decisions and plan and be more insightful. Many cultures call this wisdom and recognize how it differs from intelligence or simply knowing facts and trivia about the physical world. At the start, your inner knowing may seem very similar to instinct. A vague feeling that is difficult to describe in words, an almost automatic reaction to a situation or a person. The messages we receive from untrained instinct or psychic ability are difficult to follow and often need clarification when we look back at them after the fact. What did we feel? Was there a specific message? These psychic impressions often leave you with positive or negative emotions and not much else. As you develop your abilities, this inner knowing will slowly transition from a vague, instinctual notion to becoming more detailed, with a deeper feeling of confidence. You can pull out specifics instead of a general feeling of positive or negative energy. Why a person is acting a certain way, where a situation will lead, and how to use this knowledge to positively change your behavior and influence those around you.

Developing psychic gifts should involve the following elements:

Discovering your triggers

Psychic abilities often manifest in childhood and are often repressed soon after. Those who continue to experience psychic sensations in adulthood typically only experience them under specific conditions. First, You will need to understand when and why your abilities manifest. Is it only under stressful conditions that your intuition becomes loud enough to notice? Do you only feel clairsentience for people you trust? Or do you only see visions or images when you are in a specific environment? At first, you may have to create the conditions necessary to trigger a psychic response, and only as you discover the nature of this trigger will you be able to control when, where, and how you use your psychic abilities.

Creating your physical sanctuary

Intense concentration and focus are necessary to develop these skills. It is not easy, and you will need a space with the ideal conditions to practice. This physical space can reflect your triggers, but in all cases must be free from distraction and isolated from the psychic energy of others. Unfortunately, there is no set of rules or instructions for creating a sanctuary; it will take some experimenting on your part. Some universal things to consider are:

• Is there distracting clutter present? You do not need a plain white room, but any item that draws your mind to them or distracts your focus should be removed.

• What lighting do you need? Darkness, sunlight, a specific color, it's up to you but requires some thought and experimenting.

• How much noise can you tolerate? You can tune out street noise, or you may need noise-canceling headphones, but unlike clutter or visual distractions, it is much more difficult to remove unwanted noise.

Create a space for yourself when beginning the guided meditations as soon as possible.

Setting boundaries

As your ability to sense beyond the physical grows, the amount of energy and information you receive will increase. If you are unprepared to block some of this energy out, you may feel overwhelmed, drained, and exhausted. At the early stage of developing psychic abilities, it is important to learn to set boundaries. These include physical boundaries, for example, that nobody else is allowed in your sanctuary. Emotional boundaries, like saying no to requests from others and scheduling time for yourself. There are other types of boundaries (financial, sexual, or spiritual). Still, the key idea here is to leave enough space for your personal growth without becoming overwhelmed by others. This may feel unfair or selfish, especially if you have a partner or children, so make sure to take the time and set boundaries clearly but with compassion.

Reinforcing Abilities

Those with psychic abilities, who innately rely on intuition and creativity, often need help with this part. Reinforcing your ability takes regular dedicated practice and repetition. That will be the focus of the 11 guided meditations but will require your commitment. How far you can take your potential is up to you. Supplementing these meditations with journaling, self-care, and improving your physical health will yield the best results but will also require more time set aside for yourself.

Avoiding Negative Energy

A psychic, or psychic empath, is a living energy conduit. Developing your abilities allows energy to flow more freely through you. Unfortunately, this can also include negative energy. No discussion of developing psychic abilities is complete without a section on how to avoid, shield yourself from, or remove negative energies. There are a few basic techniques to be aware of, and you should experiment with all of them.

Grounding

Grounding is the act of releasing energy from yourself. Similar to grounding a source of electricity, you are providing your excess energy a path to flow out of your body.

The simplest way to ground yourself is to get into direct physical contact with the Earth. Stand barefoot on the grass, hug a tree, or even let sunshine wash over your face, and excess energy will flow from you into the Earth. Even just visualizing the process, imagining your feet standing on bare Earth, growing roots, and releasing extra energy back to mother earth, is often enough to remove any unnecessary buildup of psychic energy. Keep a schedule aligned with your circadian rhythm; being awake during the day, sleeping, and relaxing at night can help improve your ability to ground yourself. Having a fulfilling purpose or long-term goal also supports grounding. If there is any action or activity, like walking, creating art, or a sport or hobby you have, where you know you feel free from attachment, connection, and the energies of daily life, you can use that as a form of grounding.

Centering

Centering should be done along with grounding to have the best effect. Centering is looking deeply into your emotions and mental state and separating your mind from the external psychic energies.

What feelings are yours, and which are being channeled from others? Are you genuinely worried about something or experiencing someone else's worry?

Understanding when you feel emotions that are not yours and removing your attachment to them is a necessary skill to build.

Shielding

Shields, or barriers, are a more preventative approach. Building a spiritual barrier prevents you from absorbing too much psychic energy, and from absorbing energy when you don't wish to receive it. The most common way to create this shield is through visualization.

Imagine an almost transparent bubble or wall around you. Often people picture it as rose or blue-colored. This shield can allow positive energy in but reflects negative energy back to its source. If someone sends love or comparison, the shield lets it through; if someone else sends anger or jealousy, their negative energy is reflected back at them. It often helps to picture what energy someone, or a situation, is sending you. Intentionally imagine what type of energy is associated with certain people or interactions. A conversation over coffee with a friend might send a slow yellow glow that easily passes through your shield. Meetings with difficult coworkers might send muddy brown waves crashing against your barrier but they reflect towards their origin. Over time this visualization will become easier and also less necessary.

Avoidance

Complete avoidance may be necessary in some cases, or when other methods are ineffective. People or situations that always result in you taking in negative energy should be avoided where possible.

Dealing with narcissists, perpetual victims, dramatic people, or controlling manipulators will become even more difficult as you open your psychic channels. Be aware of any such individuals in your life and the effect they may be having on you.

11 Meditations for Empaths and Psychics

Meditation is a practice that involves focusing the mind and cultivating a state of awareness and relaxation. It is often used as a tool for spiritual development, as it can help individuals to connect with their inner selves and explore deeper spiritual experiences.

There are many different types of meditation, and the specific method best for your spiritual development will vary from person to person. Some common types of meditation that may be useful for spiritual growth include:

Mantra meditation: involves repeating a word or phrase, either out loud or silently, as a way to still the mind and connect with a higher power.

Visualization meditation: uses the power of the imagination to create vivid mental images, often as a way to connect with spiritual concepts or energies.

Loving-kindness meditation: directs feelings of love and compassion towards oneself and others to cultivate a sense of connection and understanding.

Transcendental meditation: usually requires repeating a personal mantra or word to quiet the mind and reach a state of inner peace and understanding.

Regardless of the specific method, meditation can be a powerful tool for spiritual development. It can help individuals connect with their inner selves, gain insights and understanding, and cultivate inner peace and well-being. Finding a method that works for you and being patient and consistent in your practice is important. With time and dedication, meditation becomes an integral part of your spiritual journey.

Start each of the following meditations by giving yourself five uninterrupted minutes. That might not seem like a lot, but you will gradually build up the duration or intensity of the meditation so that you can maintain your desired mental more easily. Practice the meditations on a regular basis, something that fits into your routine without adding additional stress. You should try all of the meditations, but you will have some favorites or specific skills or abilities you wish to focus on, and there is no need to try and put all eleven into your rotation. Be deliberate in how you meditate, with a clear goal on what your wish to achieve. Whether that is self-improvement, relaxation, or grounding.

Instructions, scripts, or details of the meditation will be presented in *italics*. You may wish to record yourself reading the meditation scripts, or have timers or other tools ready before beginning.

Recordings of all 11 meditations are available in the audiobook version of *Meditations for Psychics and Empaths*.

Candle meditation

Candle meditation involves focusing on a candle flame to still the mind, with the goal of cultivating a state of relaxation and internal awareness. This is a good place to start, using a simple external point of focus to ease ourselves into meditating.

Looking at the flame and following its movement can help calm the mind and bring about a sense of inner peace and clarity.

The following colors are associated with different psychic skills or emotions, and the best color to reflect your goals should be used.

White for clarity and simplicity

Blue for self-expression and communication

Purple for connection with the divine, spiritual development

Pink for warmth and love

Red for safety and grounding

Silver for clairvoyance and personal transformation

Green for healing and grounding

Here is a simple meditation that you can try starting with:

You will need a candle and a quiet, comfortable spot to practice.

Place your body into a comfortable seated position and place the candle in front of you at a comfortable distance.

Take a few slow, deep breaths and allow yourself to relax.

Gently bring your attention to the candle flame. Try to focus on the flame itself rather than any thoughts or distractions that may arise.

As you gaze at the flame, try to let go of any thoughts or worries and be present with the experience of looking at the candle.

If your mind wanders, gently bring your attention back to the candle flame. Don't jerk your attention back, just slowly and calmly refocus on the flame.

Continue to focus on the flame for as long as you like, allowing yourself to sink into a state of relaxation and inner stillness.

When you are ready to end the meditation, slowly bring your attention back to the present moment and take a few deep breaths.

When you are ready, begin your 5 minutes of meditation.

[set a timer for five minutes and begin the candle meditation]

Your 5 minutes are up. How did you do? If you were able to make it the whole 5 minutes without losing focus on the flame, consider setting a timer and extending the duration of your candle meditation next time.

Building Focus and Concentration

No we will take the candle meditation one step further. Developing your psychic and empathic abilities requires focus. A scattered mind will be unable to use these skills effectively or safely. Use the following meditation to put yourself into a focused state, ready to learn, grow, and become the person you are meant to be. Being able to maintain focus and concentration on a single idea or task is an invaluable skill and one most people today do not have. This meditation is also useful for grounding and blocking your empathic channeling if it is drawing in too much outside energy.

Extend this meditation longer once you can maintain focus for the full five minutes.

[Close your eyes gently but firmly. It feels effortless, but all outside distractions and noise are blocked.

You have created a barrier and shut out the outside world. This barrier takes no energy, requires no effort, but is impenetrable. Within this barrier is only yourself, past, present, and future.

You begin to see faint writing before you. It starts to become clear, you cannot see individual words yet, but they are coming into focus. As you see the following words, you will repeat them with your inner speech. They are now fully visible, they say:

I am alive

I am aware

I am strong

I am in control

You repeat the phrases with your inner voice, this time with confidence, knowing them to be true within this space.

I am alive

I am aware

I am strong

I am in control

Open your eyes. You can still see the phrases in writing before you. Repeat them out loud now.

I am alive

I am aware

I am strong

I am in control

Once more, with full confidence, knowing them to be true within any space and throughout every space.

I am alive

I am aware

I am strong

I am in control

Close your eyes again. The words have begun to fade, but you no longer need them

-you feel the power behind them. Repeat them once more, this time knowing they come from within yourself and you are the source of their power.

I am alive

I am aware

I am strong

I am in control

Breathe deeply, in and out, repeating the phrases with each breath; they are a part of you, your identity.

Breathe in - I am alive

Breathe out - I am aware

Breathe in - I am strong

Breathe out - I am in control

Continue this pattern. The words begin to lose meaning. They are no longer words but concepts, ideas, and energy. They are undeniable truths and have always been a part of you and will always be a part of you. The words fade from your mind, but the feelings remain. Continue deep breathing, without the words, only the essence, the feeling of each phrase. Open your eyes

You are alive

You are aware

You are strong

You are in control]

Strengthening Intuition

This is a general meditative exercise to build and trust your intuition. Being able to rely on your inner voice and hear what it is trying to tell you isn't easy for many of us, so building that trust is the focus of this exercise. Listen to the following meditation script, giving yourself at least five minutes to complete this exercise.

[You are sitting comfortably or lying down. There is no strain or stress on your body, but you do not feel sleepy or completely relaxed.

Close your eyes and focus on the sensation of your breath entering into, and then leaving your body.

As you continue to focus on your breath, all other distractions and thoughts leave your mind. Only your breath remains.

Breathe slowly but at a comfortable pace; there is no stress or strain on your body trying to breathe deeply or hold breaths. Just relaxed. In and out, focusing on that.

Continue to focus on your breath, but bring your attention to your intuition. Maybe it's a voice, a gentle pulling or pushing on you, a feeling that cannot be described with words—that part of you where your deepest thoughts and feelings originate from. Bring your intuition, whatever it feels like to you, to your attention and focus on it.

Now, ask yourself a question, or allow yourself to receive any insights or messages that come to you. Do not try to answer this question or look for specific details. Focus on your intuition and that feeling of knowledge, and remain present and open to any messages or insights that come to you without judgment or attachment.

Continue to breathe easily. You are focused on the deepest part of your inner knowledge, open to any insight, wisdom, or answers that come to you naturally, without prejudice.

Slowly and gently, take whatever knowledge you receive and begin translating it into clear thoughts. Messages from your intuition may be unclear, vague, and not have a form that can be easily translated at first. Slowly pull those ideas.

When you are ready, slowly open your eyes and take a few deep breaths.]

It may take some time and practice to develop your intuition through meditation, but with consistent practice and an open and receptive mind, you may notice an increased ability to access inner wisdom and understanding.

Building Empathy

This next exercise is focused on building empathy. If you are already an empath, this will help you consciously realize what channeling emotions feels like, so you can recognize when your emotions are not yours and centre yourself more easily. Many empaths also find this exercise helpful for managing negative channeled energy.

This meditation is longer than the previous two, so if you cannot maintain your focus for the entire length, it might be helpful to practice strengthening your focus with the candle meditation first.

[Close your eyes and feel your mind clear.

Slowly take some deep breaths. In through your nose. Out through your mouth.

Focus on your breathing, and let all other thoughts leave your mind. Visualize the air you breathe in, warming your body, filling you with strength.

Now picture someone you love. See their physical form. Their face, their eyes, their shape.

Now see the rest of their energy form. Their hopes and dreams. How it feels when you are together. How they react to you, and you to them.

On your next breath, breathe in the love you receive from this person, and breathe out the love back to them.

Breathe in the love you receive, and breathe out the love you give back.

Now breathe in and hold. Hold that love within you and feel it spread throughout your body. Feel it warm and strengthen your soul.

Breathe out again

When you are ready, picture your loved one again and breathe in the love from that person once more. Feel it spread through your body, just as it did before. But let the image of that person fade, and so only the feeling remains.

Continue holding your breath.

Now picture someone you have negative feelings towards. Continue to hold the love and energy within, but picture this other person. See how similar they are to you. They have a physical form, just like you. They have an energy form, just like you. They have feelings and thoughts and dreams, just like you.

Release your breath

We will repeat this two more times. Start by picturing someone you love and imagining them.

Breathe in their love for you, and breathe out your love back to them. When you are ready, breathe in their love, hold it within you, and picture the person you have negative feelings towards. Realize that they need love as well; they need to be understood, just like you. Now breathe out the love within you back to this other person. Even if they aren't able to receive it, or return it, continue to exhale and give back love to them.

We will repeat this one last time. Start by picturing someone you love, imagining them. Breathe in their love for you, and breathe out your love back to them. When you are ready, breathe in their love, hold it within you, and picture the person you have negative feelings towards. Realize that they need love as well; they need to be understood, just like you. Now breathe out the love within you back to this other person.

Begin to breathe normally again. You may feel drained like you have lost energy. But as your breath returns, you can picture the person you love again. They are always there, giving you love and returning energy to you.

There is no limit to this energy. No matter how much you exhale out to others, it will be returned to you. They cannot steal energy from you; it is not theirs to take.

Continue to breathe normally now. With every inhale, you are receiving love, from others, from the universe. With every exhale, you are giving love, not just to those who love you, but to everyone. This takes none of your energy; you have an unlimited supply.

You feel connected. Everyone you know is breathing in and out, sharing their energy with each other. Everyone you don't know is also connected this way, sharing their energy with each other. You can feel the swirls of energy all around you, passing through countless souls, being transformed, passed between us.

You can feel the same desire for love and acceptance in this energy; it is just expressed in different ways, transforming between people but never truly changing. You can feel the different expressions of energy from different people in your life; some are warming and loving, and some are cold and uncaring. But you understand it is all coming from the same place. The same place all people have, a common being of energy within all of us.

This idea is brought deeper into your mind, sitting within you, internalized.

You slowly open your eyes, ending the meditation when you are ready.]

Connecting to your Spirit Guide

Now that we have built up some internal strength, it is time to direct a meditation outwards and try to intentionally form a connection beyond the physical world.

Building a connection with your spirit guide takes time. Initially, you might not be able to call them, or they will appear only briefly. As you repeat this exercise, your connection will strengthen, and they will stay longer, become clearer, and may even communicate directly to you. If your spirit guide leaves early on in this meditation, slowly end it, and try again in a few days.

[Close your eyes. Gradually deepen and slow your breathing.

Breathing in for several seconds, then breathing out for several seconds.

This does not feel stressful; it is effortless, you are calm, and all thoughts leave your mind except breathing.

A picture begins to form in your mind; you are somewhere peaceful.

Somewhere you have been before and where you were happy.

You are alone in this place, but it is just as you remember it.

You can see it like you are there now. You start to notice familiar smells and sounds, and a feeling of relaxed happiness begins to fill you. You look around, recounting specific details.

As you look, you notice a door. You don't remember this door, but it belongs here. Maybe it was always there; you just never noticed. The door is closed but not locked.

You slowly approach the door. As you get closer, you can feel a warmth emanating from the door. It feels like warm sunlight, pleasant on your skin.

You now stand before the door. In your mind, you repeat the following phrases:

Spirit guide, I invite you in

Spirit guide, show yourself to me

Spirit guide, I need your help

The door opens, and a figure emerges. There is a bright light behind them. They are bathed in this light, but you can make out some details. Focus on these details and commit them to your memory.

Ask your spirit guide their name, and hold it in your memory.

Now, ask your spirit guide for their help. Your spirit guide acknowledges your request and returns back through the door. It closes softly, but you can still feel the light and warmth coming from behind it.

You are now alone again in this peaceful place. Stay here as long as you wish. When you are ready, open your eyes and end this meditation.]

Once you have finished, try to remember as many details about your spirit guide as you can. You will slowly develop a picture of them over time, gradually filling in bits and pieces of information and becoming more and more connected to them.

Kundalini - Basic Mantras

We are now going to start branching into some more technical forms of meditation. These are not necessarily more difficult, but have a more specific purpose and should not be undertaken until you feel confident in maintaining your focus.

Kundalini meditation is a spiritual practice designed to awaken and activate the kundalini energy, which is believed to be a powerful force located at the base of the spine. Kundalini meditation aims to awaken and release this energy, which is said to bring about spiritual transformation and enlightenment.

It is important to note that kundalini meditation can be a powerful and transformative practice, but it may also bring up intense emotions or physical sensations that can be difficult to process. It is important to approach kundalini meditation with caution and to seek guidance from a qualified teacher or mentor if you are interested in exploring this practice beyond these initial guided meditations. It is also important to pay attention to your physical and emotional well-being and seek medical or mental health support if needed.

Allow any physical or emotional sensations that arise during meditation to be present without judgment or attachment.

We will begin with a breathing exercise to enter an extremely relaxed meditative state. Once you have entered that state, you will stay there for at least five minutes. To help maintain your meditation, you can use any one of the following mantras either out loud or with your inner voice.

Ra Ma Da Sa Sa Se So Hang - "Sun, Moon, Earth, Infinity: All that is in infinity, I am Thee".

Ek Ong Kar - "The Creator and the Creation are one."

Ong Namo Guru Dev Namo - "I honor (or bow to) the Infinite Wisdom; I honor the teacher within.

Sat Nam - "Truth is my Identity".

Select a mantra or a short phrase meaningful to you in the current moment, then begin physically preparing yourself.

Relax; you are sitting comfortably with a straight spine.

Place your hands in your lap with your palms facing upwards.

Your shoulders are relaxed.

Let your eyes close gently, they are not shut completely, but you are unaware of your surroundings.

Begin slowing your breathing and only breathing through your nose.

Notice every part of your breath. The feeling of inhaling, your lungs filling, your chest expanding. The oxygen flowing through your body energizes it.

Exhaling is the rush of air leaving your body and releasing energy. Notice every little movement and sound you are making.

Continue to slow your breathing. Do not make it uncomfortable or hold your breath; slow down the mechanical actions of your body without any physical tension or effort.

Once you feel your have slowed your physical body as much as comfortably possible, begin your 5 minutes now, repeating your chosen mantra.

[set a timer for five minutes and repeat your chosen mantra]

It has been five minutes. Breathe in with 3 or 4 sharp breaths in a row, then breathe out with four sharp exhales in a row. Continue this pattern of breathing eight times to end your meditation.

Alpha to Theta

This next meditation is also based on principles of Kundalini meditation, and is designed to get you into a theta brain state. With slow, large amplitude brain waves the theta state will feel dream-like and allow the free flowing of intuition, representing energy being received, and creativity, representing energy being expressed or released. This is a great meditation to use as a primer for more difficult meditation exercises or before you have to complete creative or other demanding tasks.

It can be helpful to start this meditation off with five minutes of sitting quietly doing the breathing exercise of your choice beforehand.

[You are sitting quietly and comfortably.

Your eyes begin to feel heavy, and they gradually close.

You feel yourself slowly sinking backward.

As you sink backward, you can feel your mind start to clear.

You continue to relax and sink even deeper into yourself; you feel like you are slowly falling backward. As you feel yourself fall, you transition into a soft, warm space.

Relax into this space; it is safe, it is calm, and your mind is clear. You begin to notice rays of light. Faint at first, but glowing stronger and whiter with every moment. They start to shimmer and move. One of the rays is now pointed at you. You can feel it throughout your whole body. It feels like a warm, golden ray of sunshine.

Your entire body now feels like a warm light. You are no longer physical, only energy. The energy is gradually building as the rays continue to shine. The energy begins to rise.

You are weightless, a being of energy, and you are slowly leaving that warm space. Floating, rising, faster and faster. As you ascend, a being of pure energy, you expand. You are rising faster and faster, gaining more and more energy. The rays continue to fill you with powerful energy, energy that cannot be contained. Touching the world around you, extended out and up into space.

You feel more and more energy, and you begin to feel the peak approaching. You have extended out, across space, across the stars. You feel filled with beauty and wonder and are unstoppable.

You know the rays will stop soon. You can begin to feel your body again, but the warmth and energy remain. The rays of light begin to fade. But your connection, the expanse of your awareness and potential remain.

You feel the energy remaining inside you, vibrating and humming pleasantly.

Focus on that energy, and begin to direct it to your spine. As it gathers in your spine, draw it upwards. Slowly it reaches your heart, then your throat, then your eyes. Eventually, it has reached the top of your head.

Feel the energy in your spine move up and down your body with each breath. Breathe in, and the energy vibrates and charges within you. Breathe out, and the energy expands out into the universe.

You feel the familiar sensation of sinking and falling as you breathe in. As you breathe out, you remember how rising with the rays of light and energy felt.

You breathe slowly, savoring the sensations of sinking and rising. Feeling the energy course through you, under your control.

Now sit still with a clear mind.

You feel both your physical body and your pool of energy. You feel how the energy has charged your body and remains within it.

You prepare to open your eyes. You will remember the feeling of the energy in your body and how it is always there for you to tap into. You focus on this feeling and this knowledge as you gradually open your eyes. The sense of potential, vibration with the universe, and your internal power are fully part of your consciousness and identity. Your eyes are fully open, and you are aware of your surroundings again.]

Opening Chakras to Energy Flow

The chakras are centers in the body that are responsible for the flow of energy and the overall balance of the physical and emotional self. In some belief systems, it is believed that certain chakras can become blocked or closed, which can lead to physical or emotional imbalances. Meditation is a practice that involves focusing the mind and cultivating a state of awareness and relaxation. It can help open the chakras and promote the flow of energy. Here is a simple meditation that you can try to open your chakras to energy flow:

[Find a quiet, comfortable place to sit or lie down.

Take a few deep breaths, focusing on the sensation of the breath as it enters and leaves the body.

Bring your attention to the crown of your head. Visualize a glowing, white light at this point, and imagine that it is expanding and opening up to allow energy to flow in and out freely.

Move your attention down to the third eye chakra, between the eyebrows, and visualize a glowing, indigo light. Imagine that this chakra is opening and allowing energy to flow freely.

Continue moving your attention down through the other chakras, visualizing the corresponding colors. Blue in your throat, the vishuddha chakra. Green in your heart chakra. Yellow in your solar plexus. Orange below your belly button in the sacral chakra. Red in the root chakra, at the base of your spine. As you travel down through your body, imagine that they are opening, and allowing energy to flow freely.

When you reach the base of the spine, visualize all the chakras as fully open and connected, allowing energy to flow freely throughout the body.

Stay with this visualization for as long as you like, allowing yourself to sink into a state of relaxation and openness. When you are ready, slowly bring your attention back to the present moment and take a few deep breaths.]

Enhancing Intuition and Clairvoyance

This is an exercise for your third eye. It will gradually build up your intuition, with a focus on the development of clairvoyance. If you already have some degree of clairvoyance, keep that in your mind as you proceed. If you do not have any natural clairvoyant abilities, leave your mind open, reserving room in your spirit for this new ability to take hold.

[Sit in a comfortable position. You are free from distraction and focused only on your breathing. Your focus is on your lungs, pulling air in, then releasing it out. Breathing in, breathing out.

You notice nothing of the outside world, only your breath. You feel your focus slowly start to shift. Your breath continues, but your focus slowly travels upwards. Moving upwards past your heart, continuing through your throat, then slowing as it passes into your head. Slowing and settling between your eyebrows, then gently falling back into the center of your head, stopping.

Aligning with your third eye. It feels natural; there is a natural point of focus here, and it belongs and feels comfortable. As you continue to breathe and feel energy pass into your body, then release from your body, you can feel your third eye resonate. You can feel your third eye begin to awaken. Continue to focus on this point between your eyebrows in the center of your head. If you lose focus, pull back to this point.

You can feel the power within this point. It is not an energy of strength or control; it is an energy of connection. Through this point, you are connected to everything. You can see all those connected to you, the links between people, between realms, and between times.

Keep your focus on this point, but feel the connections surrounding it. As you continue to focus, imagine your third eye growing stronger. This strength comes from the connections it has, the links it has with others.

You begin to notice the rest of your body again. Your focus begins to shift again; it begins to move downwards, slowly moving to the base of your skull. As your focus leaves your third eye, it begins to fade from your mind. The sensation of connection starts to fade, but you remember the strength behind it. Those connections remain present; they do not fade; you are just no longer consciously aware of them. Your focus passes out of your head and travels down your neck, then into your lungs.

You continue breathing, ending the meditation when you are ready.]

Psychic Development

This breath training must be done with a clear state of mind free from judgment, self-doubt, fear, or any other negative energy. It focuses purely on psychic development, but this meditation will be more effective if you have a clear goal.

What skill are you trying to improve or develop? How do you want it to feel? Are you seeking more clarity from your senses, more frequent glimpses of knowledge?

During this exercise you will imagine your future state, weeks, months, or years from now, and picture a path between here and there. This exercise will bring you one step further along that path. Hold this vision in your subconscious mind as you follow the breathing pattern.

[Sit down in a comfortable position, with your back straight and feet grounded on the floor.

Hold up your hands and examine your ten fingers. Place your thumbs over your ears, your index and middle finger over your brow, connecting at your third eye. Place your ring fingers on your nostrils and your pinkies in the crease of your lips. This position is for a breathing exercise, where you will breathe in for 5 seconds, hold for 5 seconds, breathe out over 5 seconds, then hold for 5 seconds. During this time you will picture the path of your psychic development, what skills you will develop, what abilities you will harness, and how you will grow spiritually.

Breathe in 2, 3, 4, 5, 6, 7, 8

Hold 2, 3, 4, 5, 6, 7, 8

Release 2, 3, 4, 5, 6, 7, 8

Hold 2, 3, 4, 5, 6, 7, 8

Breathe in 2, 3, 4, 5, 6, 7, 8

Hold 2, 3, 4, 5, 6, 7, 8

Release 2, 3, 4, 5, 6, 7, 8

Hold 2, 3, 4, 5, 6, 7, 8

Continue with this breathing pattern.]

Manifest Your Purpose

This meditation will cover five separate concepts here, and you will give each of them one minute of undivided attention and focus. Concentrate and repeat these questions regularly, either individually or during this five-minute sequence.

Over time, you should build up a detailed vision of your purpose. This vision can guide the development of your psychic abilities, so you can focus on what is truly important to you and discard what is merely a distraction.

[*Identifying your values*: What is important to you? What do you believe in? Think deeply about your values and how they could be reflected in the purpose and direction of your life.

Setting goals: What do you most want to achieve? What is the most important step in reaching that goal? Focus on what you want to accomplish and what give you a sense of purpose and motivation.

Taking action: Once you have identified your values and set goals, it is important to take action to work towards them. This can involve planning and taking small, consistent steps toward your goals. What is the next task you can complete that aligns with your values and will move your towards your goals?

Reflecting and reassessing: Reflect on your progress and whether your goals and actions align with your values and purpose. What adjustments do you need to make to stay on track?

Seeking support: Is there someone in your circle you can help you find and maintain purpose in your life? Is there any additional support you need along your journey, and where could you find it?

Your meditation is complete. As you continue to focus on your breath, you might repeat a mantra or phrase to yourself, such as "I am focused and determined" or "I am open to success and growth." Use that phrase whenever you feel unsure of your next action or next steps in your journey.]

Conclusion

May these meditations help you reach your goals, find the peace we are all looking for, and improve your mental health. Use these meditations as tools to support you on your journey towards your true purpose.

Affirmations for Empaths and Psychics

Setting aside enough time to practice meditation regularly can be difficult. As a bonus with that reality in mind, here is a collection of mantras that may be helpful for empaths to use as a form of self-care and self-protection. These can be repeated in times of stress or as a form of quick grounding or utilized repetitively in a longer meditation session to reinforce this idea in your mind more strongly.

"I am responsible for my own emotions."

"I have the power to set healthy boundaries."

"I am strong and capable of handling difficult emotions."

"I am worthy of love and respect."

"I am safe and protected."

Using these mantras, or creating your own, can be a helpful way to remind yourself of your strength and boundaries and to practice self-compassion and self-care. It is important for empaths to take care of their emotional well-being and to set boundaries to prevent burnout and maintain a healthy and balanced life.

Affirmations are positive statements intended to help individuals focus their thoughts and beliefs in a specific direction. They are often used to help individuals develop new skills or behaviors or to overcome negative thought patterns. Here are a few examples of affirmations that could potentially be used to help develop psychic ability:

"I am open and receptive to my psychic abilities."

"I trust in my own intuitive abilities."

"I am confident in my ability to connect with my higher self and access my psychic gifts."

"I am willing to practice and develop my psychic abilities."

"I am attuned to my own inner wisdom and can access it at any time."

Select one that resonates with you, or write your own to repeat whenever you have a few minutes to spare or need to refocus your mind.

Book Three
Protection and Reversal Spells

Introduction

The witch community is filled with the brightest, most creative, and most welcoming people I know. For many new witches, discovering their limitless potential and the beauty of the truth behind witchcraft is a life-changing experience. But magic is a natural force and does not belong to witches or any belief system.

Magic is an intrinsic part of reality that everybody has some degree of access to. And while the witch community does its best to bring forth positive intent and use magic to make the world a better place, not everyone shares these ideals. Even people completely unaware of their spiritual energy can influence the spirit realm. Actions and thoughts in the physical realm are reflected in the spiritual realm, even with no conscious intention behind them. Sources of negative energy and spiritual ill intent do exist, and we must be prepared to face them.

There are also those who practice witchcraft who have strayed from finding their true purpose and experimenting with black magic, either for selfish reasons such as material gain or to actively harm others. Being targeted by black magic is serious, and while it rarely

INTRODUCTION

happens in the witch community, it is important to be aware of this possibility.

Another source of negative energy is one most witches will eventually come across. As part of any journey of self-discovery, you will come to a point where there is internal resistance, self-sabotage, or deep-rooted ill intent you are not consciously aware of. Having darker thoughts, negative emotions, or selfish desires doesn't make you a bad person. But as you become more powerful, you must ensure that these shadows within you don't become more powerful.

As witches grow in skill and experience and begin to experience the spiritual realm more fully, they can be more susceptible to the negative energies that exist there, either from external or internal sources. You can't receive the good without protecting yourself against the bad.

For every creative thought or positive emotion that flows toward you now, you may have to redirect or block a few negative thoughts or harmful ideas. This is normal, and while it can be unpleasant, as long as you prepare yourself properly, you can experience all of the benefits of witchcraft with none of the drawbacks. Look at this aspect of witchcraft as a positive; as you learn to defend and protect yourself from spiritual damage, this will be reflected in your physical self, and you will become stronger and more resilient. In the same way learning self-defense will make you more confident physically; learning protection and reversal magic will make you more confident spiritually.

Curses and Hexes

It is impossible to determine with certainty whether or not someone has been cursed. But if you suspect that your body, mind, or spirit has been attacked, there are a few symptoms to watch for:

- repeated nightmares with similar topics or imagery,
- persistent feelings of unsettledness, unexplained fatigue,
- behaving out of character, or
- if you notice your electronics or appliances are malfunctioning for no reason.

Curses can be applied in many different ways.

Cursed objects, or hexes, are objects that have been imbued with negative energy or that have been the focus of a curse. Being close to a cursed object, especially one spiritually connected to you can be dangerous.

The evil eye is a curse believed to be caused by someone who gives someone else a look of envy or malice, causing them to suffer bad luck or other negative consequences.

Voodoo dolls or hex dolls are a type of cursed object that is believed to be able to cause harm to a person or bring about negative events when it is manipulated in certain ways.

A **jinx** is a curse or hex placed on a person and believed to bring about bad luck or negative events.

A **hex bag** is a small bag believed to contain cursed objects or substances. It is used to bring about negative events or circumstances.

Unwanted spirits may be present and attached to you without your consent.

Psychic attacks

A psychic attack is a term used to describe the belief that an individual's energy or well-being is negatively affected by another person's intentional or unintentional actions. While curses and hexes often target your well-being in the physical realm, black magic can also be used to harm others in the spirit realm.

This can manifest as energy blockages, a flood of negative emotions that overwhelm shields, or an inability to ground yourself properly. Psychic attacks are most often felt when performing magic or during dreams.

Dispelling Black Magic and Negative Energy

Suppose you are concerned that you may have been cursed. In that case, it is important to remember that it is natural to experience ups and downs in life and that negative events or circumstances can occur for various reasons. Immediately assuming anything bad that happens is due to negative energy or black magic will put you into a mindset that inhibits your spiritual growth.

The effects of black magic are often subtle and indirect, such as a chain of unfortunate events or disproportionately bad luck over a long period. While stronger black magic can result in direct harm, such as injury or illness, with no apparent cause, this is rare. There are a few key methods for dealing with black magic used intentionally against you or negative energies harming you.

Types of Protection Spells and Traditional Cures

Wards, shields, and barriers prohibit negative energy or harmful magic from crossing thresholds or personal boundaries.

Reflections return negative energy or magic to their source or direct it into the earth, where it is neutralized.

Camouflage spells work by hiding the target from outside magical forces.

Reversal spells transform the negative energy, using it to power other forms of positive or white magic.

Praying or asking for **divine intervention** to lift the curse, your guardian spirit is a great place to start.

Seeking the assistance of a **healer, shaman, or other spiritual leader** who is believed to have the ability to lift curses.

This type of magic can be cast using protective charms or amulets with herbs, crystals, or other natural substances. It may use various rituals or ceremonies to counter black magic's effects directly. They can also be done as a precaution to cleanse sacred areas or purify the energy of a person or space.

Reversal magic

A reversal spell is a type of magic spell that is used to reverse or undo the effects of a previous spell. Their most common use is to undo the effects of other harmful spells or curses or to counter the influence of negative energies. They may also be used to reverse the effects of spells cast to cause harm or cause someone to act against their will, even if you were not personally the target of these actions.

Dispelling Black Magic and Negative Energy

Setting Boundaries

Traditional cures and reversal magic are useful for dispelling black magic, but what if the negative energy affecting you was not intentionally cast? People who unintentionally send negative energy your way can often be best dealt with by setting boundaries.

It is important to be aware of your physical, emotional, and energetic boundaries and to take steps to protect them. Knowing what people you are channeling negative energy from or which environments or situations cause you to accumulate negative energy is important. This self-awareness is critical to protecting yourself properly. This can involve limiting your time with certain individuals, setting clear boundaries around personal space and privacy, and learning to say no to requests or invitations that do not align with your values or needs.

Taking care of your physical and emotional well-being can help build resilience and protect you from negative energy. This can involve engaging in activities that nourish the mind, body, and spirit, such as exercise, meditation, or creative pursuits.

Boundary spells and symbols

Take the idea of setting boundaries to the next level. These spells are designed to protect unwanted energy or spirits from entering thresholds. Ancient versions of these are known as 'witch marks.'

These marks, usually carved into entrances and thresholds, were used to turn away evil. Most protective spells work in a similar way by protecting thresholds, either physical ones, entrances to places or your body, or spiritual thresholds.

Visualization and Affirmations

These actions can be used more as a regular maintenance activity. A regular flush of negative energy from your system is a precaution to ensure that it isn't building up over time. Keeping yourself spiritually healthy will also allow you to handle any large influx of negative energy or black magic more effectively.

Some people find it helpful to use visualization or affirmations to create a protective shield or bubble around themselves. This can involve visualizing a protective light or energy surrounding you or repeating affirmations such as "I am protected and safe."

The Rule of Threefold Return

When we are attacked, magically or otherwise, our first instinct might be to strike back. If you are new to witchcraft and its core beliefs, you might feel the desire to use your abilities to right any wrongs done to you. Before we get to details of the protection and reversal spells, let's do a quick refresher on the rule of threefold return—a fundamental principle of Wiccan philosophy but one shared in most traditional forms of witchcraft.

This rule states that any energy, intention, or effect you put into the universe, spiritually or physically, will be returned to you threefold. This principle holds true in both the spiritual and physical realms, and there is no way around it, no shortcuts, and no loopholes. In everything you do, big or small, the universe will return your intent back to you. Similar to the conservation of energy, any action or energy put out into the world is never used up or destroyed, only transformed, and your actions as a witch, transforming the energy of the universe, have consequences.

Good intentions and acts of kindness to others will multiply and improve your situation. Acts of aggression, selfishness, and those borne out of fear, jealousy, or other negative emotions will also be returned to you even more strongly. This is more than just the ethics of using magic for good or evil; this is the realization that the intent you put into the universe can have repercussions on you, that the interconnectedness of all of our spirits means any harm done to others is even more harmful to ourselves.

While the law of threefold return is often attributed directly to the modern Wiccan movement developed by Gerald Gardener, similar concepts and teachings are present in almost all forms of traditional witchcraft. Whether you specifically call it karma, divine reciprocity, or some other term, there is a natural system of balance in the universe that all practitioners of witchcraft must consider. It is not a mathematical formula where you can calculate the exact amount of harm or good your actions are doing; the world is much too complex to quantify anything. The best we can hope for is to act responsibly, as best we can, and be mindful in all aspects of our lives.

So back to protection and reversal spells. If we believe we have been wronged or are under physical or spiritual attack, we can rightfully defend ourselves. But with the understanding of the threefold rule, we do not need to punish our attackers directly or lash out and continue a cycle of aggression or negative behavior. Several of the spells in the following chapter require careful consideration of the rule of threefold return before they can be safely cast. Considering your deeper intent behind your actions and whether they are helping you on your journey to find your true purpose and self.

The Rule of Threefold Return

Finally, before we begin learning specific spells, there is no way to *fight fire with fire* when dealing with black magic. The appropriate counter to a black spell, curse, or hex is always white magic.

11 Protection and Reversal Spells

These spells are suitable for a new witch, but many require a few basic materials and at least some experience with spells. They will allow you to act and protect yourself against negative energy being consciously or unconsciously directed at you, or from your fears and internal struggles. While knowing various forms of protection and reversal magic is highly recommended, some types of spells will be more suited to your personality, style, and magical affinity. Once you have discovered which spells resonate with you or are most relevant to your life, you can start looking for more advanced teachings.

Preventative Protection Charms

Let's start with something fundamental, something every witch should know and should be doing at all times. As a preventative measure against negative energy and spirits, you can carry a small bag of sea salt with you. Salt is a powerful protective agent and can be used in many ways to ward off evil spirits. Additionally, you can place a bowl of salt near the front door of your home; or you could take this a step further and place some salt on the threshold of each room and near windows for protection against spirits and bad luck. Using salt to prevent negative energy, spirits, and curses from crossing thresholds is the most basic form of protection magic but also one of the most effective.

There are other basic forms of protective charms; here are some easy examples you can use:

- A symbol or talisman representing your guardian spirit;
- A sigil of your own creation that symbolizes protection;
- Charging a piece of jewelry or other item with magical energy, intending to be used as a protective charm.

If you choose to use a non-magical item as a protection charm, you must purify it and dispel any existing energy before charging it yourself. Once charged, this item can no longer be used for its original purpose and should be considered a magical tool.

11 Protection and Reversal Spells

Home Blessing

This spell will protect any space you consider a home, whether a house, apartment or even a single room. This spell works best when combined with smudging, the burning of sacred magical ingredients, often herbs. The choice of smudging ingredients is up to you but should include equal elements of earth, fire, air, and water.

Herbs have specific meanings, so consult a herbal grimoire to select the most relevant to the dangers you are trying to prevent or remove. If you need access to herbs, or if you are still getting familiar with smudging, you can try the spell only as an incantation. Or, if another school of magic is more your style, you can substitute smudging for the magical tools of your choice, such as crystals, sigils, or candles. Just remember to try and keep to the same balance of equal parts earth, fire, air, and water.

If you are going to try smudging and aren't familiar with herbal magic, here are some common herbs of each element:

Earth herbs: alfalfa, cumin, patchouli, sea salt, wormwood

Fire herbs: allspice, garlic, mustard, pine, tarragon

Air herbs: fennel, lavender, lemon grass, oregano, sage, thyme

Water herbs: cardamom, catnip, elm, hibiscus, poppy seed, sandalwood

To cast this spell, burn the herbs in the center of your home. Make sure there are no closed doors or barriers within the space you consider home, and close any external thresholds, such as doors and windows, to properly contain the spell. Once you are ready, recite this incantation:

Strength of stone and fire from the earth,
Bring protection to this home and hearth.

Swirling air and flowing waters,
Bless all these dwellings, sons and daughters.

Drive away all harm and fear,
For only good may enter here.

This spell can be repeated multiple times over a period of days to reinforce it and should be cast monthly to prevent the magical effect from fading.

Banishment

If you suspect an evil spirit has become attached to you, regardless of how it happened, this spell will remove them from your physical and spiritual presence. Stronger spirits may require several repetitions to complete the banishment. If you are still a beginner and believe a spirit has become attached to you but are not sure, here are some signs to look for:

- hearing strange voices or feeling sensations of cold;
- having intrusive thoughts or compulsions;
- experiencing repeated nightmares;
- noticing unfamiliar and unpleasant spells around you;
- newfound fears, anxieties, or phobias.

If these symptoms become serious, please consult an experienced practitioner and your medical health professional.

To cast the spell, write these words on paper, light a flame, burn the paper to ash, then blow out the flame toward a doorway or threshold. After banishing negative energy, spread some form of salt along the threshold to prevent it from returning to you.

Evil spirits within our plane,
Leave and return whence you came.

With Hecate's torch, I banish thee,
And cleanse this circle's energy.

Free from evil, malice, and harm,
With peace and charity from this charm.

Karmic Retribution

There are potential grey areas in witchcraft, and while at first glance this spell may seem to be asking for harm to come to a spiritual or magical attacker, it is your intent behind it which will determine if it crosses the line into black magic. Cast this spell with the intention that you wish no direct harm to the target; you only wish for the rule of threefold return to be justly applied, strengthening the sympathetic metaphysical link between the target and whomever you believe them to have harmed. It is not your intent to create a direct magical effect here, only to ensure that the spiritual damage done by others does not go unnoticed and is karmically reflected in the physical realm.

Repeat the following with a calm state of mind, not wishing any specific consequences, and allowing the cosmos to render their judgment. Focus not on the target of their spell but on the pain or damage caused by their actions instead.

Wait at least three days after the malicious action by the target before acting.

> *Nemesis, I call to your attention,*
> *Actions of malice and ill intention.*
>
> *Corruption of sacred magick and trust,*
> *Spirits coerced for actions unjust.*
>
> *I come to you pure of soul and mind,*
> *Asking no vengeance or pain in kind.*
>
> *Render justice through the karmic wheel,*
> *With the rule of three, their fate to seal.*

11 Protection and Reversal Spells

Clearing Negative Internal Thoughts

Negative thoughts are a normal part of life. Still, if they are persistent and start interfering with your well-being or spiritual growth, finding ways to clear them from your mind may be helpful.

As you become more attuned to the spirit realm and energies of others during your development as a witch, you may find yourself more susceptible to negative energy and could inadvertently start channeling it.

Here are a few tips that may help clear negative thoughts if simple grounding activities are not sufficient. First, you must actively recognize when you are having negative thoughts. Pay attention to your state of mind and try to identify patterns or triggers contributing to your negative thinking. Once you have recognized the negative thought, you must challenge it. When you have a negative thought, try to evaluate whether it is based on fact, or whether it is an irrational belief or from an external source. If the thought is not truly your own, try to replace it with more balanced or realistic thoughts. Ask yourself if the thoughts are your own or if they originated externally. Channeling the negative thoughts and beliefs of others can be extremely draining.

This practice requires no additional items or magical tools. Start by breathing in and out slowly three times to set your protection spell. When you are calm and centered, chant the following protection spell three times:

Elements of the day,
Come forth this way.

Elements of the night,
Turn towards me your sight.

Powers of the Night and Day, I now summon thee,
Come to my aid, and with your strength, please protect me.

This is a powerful and protective spell that has been in practice by occultists, witches, and believers for many centuries. Connecting deeply to your innate sense of protection while chanting this spell will help solidify your intention. Try to imagine a ball of golden energy surrounding you while you chant this spell, growing stronger with each reciting.

11 Protection and Reversal Spells

Recharge and Cleanse your Aura

This ritual will fully recharge your aura and is useful when you feel especially drained. A purifying bath that recharges both the physical and spiritual.

Depending on the type of witchcraft you practice, you might know some additional items to add to supplement the steps here. Herbs or oils as a kitchen witch, gemstones as a crystal witch, or even just incorporating natural elements, colors, and specific numbers of items.

To prepare the ritual, you will need Epsom salts, dried rosemary, and sandalwood essential oil.

Method:

- Mix the ingredients in a small bowl.
- Set your intention. This might be "I am protected and relaxed" or "I feel peaceful and recharged".
- Draw a bath and sprinkle the Epsom salt blend under the running water.
- Visualize your intention as you soak in the bath.
- Soak as long as you like. When you're done, imagine all negative energy flowing down the drain along with the bathwater.
- Remember, as with all spell work, you need to be focused specifically on the intent of "protection" for your spells and rituals to have the greatest effect.

Requesting Protection from Psychic Attacks

Psychic attacks often happen while you are asleep, when your link to the spirit world is strongest and you are the least able to protect yourself. These attacks can be felt as nightmares, disturbances in sleep, or feelings of fatigue even after a full night's rest. Dreams allow us to connect to our inner wisdom, and anything that disturbed this connection can cause more damage than we may realize.

This spell requests protection for your spirit guide while you sleep, and will also help you remember your dreams. Being more aware of your subconscious will allow you to better protect yourself, and notice when negative energies are infiltrating your life. Repeat this mantra before sleeping:

Spirit guide your help I seek,
To watch over me while I sleep.

Follow me into my dreams tonight,
Keep them full of love and light.

Allow no energy or spirit unkind,
To disturb me wandering through my mind.

Let me remember my thoughts and visions,
So tomorrow I retain my subconscious wisdom.

Additional dream work can be helpful for most practitioners. As a start, try keeping a dream journal near your bedside and try to record whatever you remember from your dreams as soon as you wake every day.

11 Protection and Reversal Spells

Crystal Magic for Protection

Keeping specific crystals or stones for protection is a common strategy for witches. They can not only repel negative energy, they can also help remove that negative energy from your body and aura.

The slow natural vibrations of crystals help keep your environment balanced and peaceful, acting as a steady and long-lasting deterrent to negative energies and spirits. There are several protection crystals to choose from.

Obsidian: absorbs negative energy and can shield you from psychic and emotional attacks. This is the most common protection crystal and considered the most powerful, and is able to shield your aura from anxiety, stress, and any recurring negative thoughts. Obsidian is commonly worn in jewelry.

Black Tourmaline: actively repels negative energy from other people. This crystal excels at grounding and will help you feel recharged. Keep it with you while you are in public spaces or around large groups of people.

Citrine and Amethyst: protect against physical ailments, as well as pain relief and sleep disturbances. This crystal is more of a boost to your own positive energy than a block on negative energy, but will have a similar effect. Use citrine while meditating to facilitate the flow of positive energy, and keep amethyst by your bedside.

Clear quartz: is one of the most common crystals, and has many uses in witchcraft. Often used as an amplifier in other spells, combining crystal quartz with any other protection spell can make the spell more powerful and effective.

Selenite: is known for its high vibrational energy, making it an ideal protective shield. This crystal is best used for home protection, or creating psychic shields. Place the selenite in the space you wish to protect, or use a selenite lamp to keep an area free from negative energy.

Tiger's Eye: is not necessarily a protective crystal, but will increase your confidence, awareness, and determination. The effects of this crystal can often counteract any negative energy or spiritual attacks on you.

11 Protection and Reversal Spells

Camouflage Spell

Spells like these not only help you escape the notice of negative energy or malevolent spirits, they can also help you be less visible in the physical realm. We have all had periods where we wish to go unnoticed or more easily blend in to our surroundings, or have our aura less visible to others.

This is a moon spell and if possible should be cast with the appropriate phase of the moon. If the camouflage is associated with a fresh start or keeping hidden, cast during a new moon. If the camouflage spell is for ending a phase of your life, transitioning, or banishing cast during a waxing moon. Cast this spell while outside and facing the moon, invoking the moon goddess Selene.

Selene look upon me and hear my cry,
Bring forth a blessing, brightness from the sky,

Hide my essence from those bringing harm,
Bestow on me secrecy with this lunar charm.

Grounded Reflection Spell

Reflecting energy or spells can be difficult, and for these spells to be effective, your energy needs to be fully centered and grounded. Think of this grounding spell as strengthening your foundation or roots, so that when you are targeted by a spell you are not as influenced by it, you can stand your ground and easily redirect it.

Grounding spells are best performed outdoors, with a direct connection to the ground. If that isn't possible for you, touching stone, a large tree, or other natural object can have a similar effect. Once you are in position, feeling comfortable and relaxed, recite the following:

As I recite this heartfelt speech,
Deep into the earth my spirit shall reach,

Receiving wisdom and strength from the earth, our mother,
Please guard my spirit against harm from any other,

I shall not bend, or break, my energy is kept,
As spells, curses, and dark energy must reflect,

No harm may come, all evil shall pass,
I am one with the sun, the wind, and the grass.

If you have your own grounding or centering rituals, you should perform them first before completing this incantation.

11 Protection and Reversal Spells

Protection and Reversal Mantras

If you find that constantly trying to keep up a protective shield or wall around yourself is using up too much of your energy, here are some short mantras you can try. Repeat these on a regular basis as part of a daily routine, and you may find them to be just as effective as casting more involved spells.

When you initially select one or two of the mantras below, read them slowly to yourself. Make sure they resonate with your energy and are meaningful to you. If you need to make small adjustments to the wording, then do so. There is no need to make long or complex phrases, keep things simple, so you can immediately direct your intention and focus with minimal effort.

The first time you recite the mantra take your time, and do so with your intention focused on safeguarding your spirit and energy. If you can sit comfortably in the lotus position, do so. Remember the feeling that flowed through your body as you said the words out loud, and recite the mantra again. Pause, take a minute or two to refocus, imagining the effect it will have on your body and mind, and recite it a final time.

I am in control of my energy.

I am safe and secure.

I am grounded, calm, and cannot be harmed.

I am connected to my spirit guardian and under their protection.

I am free of negative thoughts and will act to further my true purpose.

Once you have fully ingrained the importance of your chosen mantra into your subconscious, it will retain some degree of effectiveness simply when spoken even without focused intent. This magical shorthand can be helpful if you are often surprised or are caught off-guard in situations where your spiritual energy is vulnerable.

Conclusion

Use these tools wisely and purposefully. So that nothing may stop you on your journey to discover your true purpose. Whether from outside or within, you now have every tool you need to remove the barriers that have been holding you back, slowing you down, or testing your resolve.

Printed in Great Britain
by Amazon